SOME ELEMENTS OF RELIGION

SOME ELEMENTS OF RELIGION

Lent Lectures

1870

BY

H. P. LIDDON, D.D.

CANON OF ST. PAUL'S

NEW YORK

SCRIBNER, WELFORD, & ARMSTRONG

1872

Perchè, se tu alla virtù circonde
La tua misura, non alla parvenza
Delle sustanzie che t' appaion tonde,
Tu vederai mirabil convenenza,
Di maggio a più, et di minore a meno,
In ciascun cielo, a sua intelligenza.

PAR. xxviii. 73—78.

TO

John William Ogle, Esq., M.D.

OF TRINITY COLLEGE, OXFORD

WHOSE WORK AND CHARACTER SUGGEST

MANY PRECIOUS LESSONS

WHICH HE NEVER THINKS OF

TEACHING

ADVERTISEMENT.

These Lectures were delivered in St. James' Church, Piccadilly, during the Lent of 1870.

They were, at the time, through God's mercy, of service at least to some minds,—anxious, if it might be, to escape from perplexities which beset an age of feverish scepticism. It was accordingly difficult to resist the practical reasons which were urged in favour of publishing the Lectures; but the announcement of their intended publication was, perhaps, made, before the drawbacks which must necessarily accompany the rhetorical treatment of such a subject as the present, in a permanent form, had been sufficiently considered. Moreover, a fulness and method of discussion which satisfies the purposes of a Lecture, and which indeed is all that an audience will bear, must fall altogether below the standard which may be reasonably looked for in a book, supposed to make any pretension whatever to claim the character of a formal treatise upon a wide and serious subject. Of this, upon further reflection, the writer became so strongly convinced as to have entertained the design of expanding these fragments into a larger work. But, apart from the pressure of other duties, he could not but feel that such an attempt would destroy, together with the identity of the Lectures, any moral or spiritual associations that might cling to them; and, in working for the cause of Faith, as in other matters,

> " Un sou, quand il est assuré,
> Vaut mieux, que cinq en espérance."

The Lectures are therefore published as they stand. It will be borne in mind that they suggest only a few thoughts on each of the points of which they treat; that they cannot but raise some difficulties which they leave unanswered; and, in a word, that their limits are not in any sense determined by those of the general subject, but only by the number of Sundays in Lent.

WHITSUNTIDE, 1872.

CONTENTS

LECTURE IV.

Fourth Sunday in Lent.

THE OBSTACLE TO RELIGION—SIN.

LECTURE V.

Fifth Sunday in Lent.

PRAYER, THE CHARACTERISTIC ACTION OF RELIGION.

LECTURE VI.

Palm Sunday.

THE MEDIATOR, THE GUARANTEE OF RELIGIOUS LIFE.

LECTURE I.

First Sunday in Lent.

THE IDEA OF RELIGION.

Ps. cxliii. 8.

Shew Thou me the way that I should walk in, for I lift up my soul unto Thee.

OUR age, it has been said, longs to be religious. If this is too unguarded an assertion, it is at least true that the instinct or sentiment of religion is treated among us with more respect and sympathy than has been the case at some past epochs of our national history. Amid the debaucheries of the Restoration, and the shallow habits of thought on the gravest subjects which marked portions of the last century, Religion, in the broad sense of the term, was largely discredited, even when it was not openly scouted as a weakness or a superstition. Whereas in our day religion is named, even by the irreligious, with the forms if not with the sincerity of respect. And some men interest themselves in religion as an abstract good, with very great sincerity, who oppose by turns all that asserts its power and presence in the world. Thus they declaim against churches, while they explain that in doing this they are befriending that true Religion which churches misrepresent. Or, they would do away with priesthoods; but then they are only anxious, while rescuing the fair jewel of religion from clerical keeping, to make its sway more imperial, by making its mien and countenance more human. Or they make war upon theology—the theology of Apostles, Fathers, Creeds; but theology, they declare, again and again, is a pedantic product of the clerical understanding, and they for their part are passionately interested on behalf of the religion of the human heart. They discredit "book revelations," and insist upon errors of fact or errors of morals, which they hold to be discoverable in the Bible; but they are all the more eager to profess and feel a zeal for that unerring and sublime essence of religion, which is not bound, as they phrase it, to the letter, and which fires their enthusiasm in renouncing the letter. And thus, however warmly the institutions, the ministers, the beliefs, the sacred literature of religion, may be successively assailed, religion itself, we are assured, is respected; or rather it is respect for and loyalty to religion—to religion divested of accretions which have gathered round it and obscured its beauty during the lapse of time,—which is in fact the animating motive of this most friendly and discriminating opposition.

That religion should be thus safeguarded as an idea, when all that secures its practical power is by turns objected to; that the abstract, disembodied, intangible essence should be so sedulously honoured, while its concrete forms, its living and working embodiments, are opposed and denounced, is a fact which must engage attention. How are we to account for it? Is it that we live in a "period of transition," when men have not yet faced the last consequences of the principles which they are adopting, and hang with a pardonable, although illogical tenderness between premiss and conclusion? Does the sacred name of religion still command an awe which, while it is not strong enough to protect many practical interests, can yet hedge around a remote object with the forms of popular respect? Is it that, as of old, barbarian invaders, who will without scruple devastate the precincts and sack the interior of the temple, are pausing involuntarily, spell-bound, almost terrified, upon the threshold of the sacred shrine? Or does the æsthetic feeling of our time, looking at human life with the eye of an artist rather than with the eye of a statesman or philanthropist, prompt this interest on behalf of religion, as alone adequately representing and upholding the ideal side of human existence? Does it anticipate, not without reason, the dull, barren, uninteresting, prosaic level of existence to which we should be reduced, if all that points upward in thought and feeling could be utterly stripped from us, and eliminated; if human life could be robbed of the most refining and stimulating influences that can be brought to bear on it? Or is this reserve of interest on behalf of religion at bottom a social, or political—if you like, a selfish—class instinct? Is it order cowering before approaching revolution, and endeavouring to support its regiments and its policemen with forces summoned from some higher world, whether of fact or fancy; with invisible powers capable of making their way into the very heart of the enemy's camp? Is it that we of this generation, who have read in the annals of a neighbouring country the stern lessons taught by eighty years of active or suppressed anarchy, are more keenly alive than were our ancestors to the tremendous force of the volcanic passions latent in human nature? Are we willing to grant that some religion at least is a social necessity; a necessity in the sense of Machiavelli, if not in the sense of Jesus Christ? Are we satisfied that the brute within us, if he is to be chained and imprisoned at all, can only be taken captive by a superhuman master, and will never forfeit his destructive liberty, except at the bidding of an unearthly creed?

Undoubtedly, it may be admitted that religion owes something, on the score of respect yielded to her as an abstract idea, to each of these causes. The awe which a reasoned scepticism cannot always crush, the perception of what it is that constitutes beauty in life, combine with the stern practical instincts of social safety, with the love of order, and the anxiety to make property and life secure, to insist that man must have something in the way of a religion. Schemes of independent morality, even if they were theoretically defensible, are not equal to resisting the impetuosities of passion, or the exorbitant demands of a low self-interest. "Take my word for it," said a great statesman, "it is not prudent as a rule to trust yourself to any man who tells you that he does not believe in a God or in a future after death."[1]

But a deeper reason for the fact we are considering, is to be found in the wider conviction that religion is, if I may so express it, an indispensable part of man's moral and mental outfit. Two causes have contributed to deepen this conviction in modern times.

The first is the subjective spirit of the age, which insists on looking at truth, not as it is in itself, in its utter independence of the mind of man, but as it presents itself to man's mind, or rather as man's mind in very varying moods apprehends it. This spirit, while it has weakened the public hold upon Creeds and Scriptures, has directed attention, with an intensity unknown before our day, to the needs of the human mind, and among them to its supreme need of a religion. It has indeed exaggerated this into maintaining, as with Feuerbach, that all existing religions are but the creations of human thought, which, while it is really doomed to an uninterrupted contact with the world of sense, aspires to create, if it cannot discover, an ideal world beyond; but this paradox only yields an additional testimony to the need we have, as men, of some religion, in order to do justice to our humanity. Religion, says a modern English writer, who certainly will not be suspected of any desire to exaggerate its influence, is that "which gives to man, in the midst of the rest of creation, his special

[1] Sir Robert Peel.

elevation and dignity."[1] And it was perhaps, upon the whole, the most marked feature in the work of Schleiermacher, that when groping his way back from the grim intellectual desert into which many of his countrymen had been led, under the guidance of the older Rationalism, he insisted with such emphasis and success upon the necessity of religion in order to the completion of human life. Beyond any of his contemporaries, he saw and pointed out that by our capacity for religion; by our power of looking beyond this deceptive and passing world of sense to a higher world, invisible and eternal; by loyalty to the obligations which that clearer sight imposes on us, we men are best distinguished from the brutes around us. Language itself, the physical dress in which we clothe our thought, is not more distinctly royal among our outward human prerogatives, than that upturned countenance which, as the heathen poet divined, is the symbol of our intelligent capacity for a higher life.

The indispensableness of religion to human life has also been forced on the mind of this generation by a deeper study of history. The more we know of the annals of our race, the more clearly is it seen how the greatest catastrophes, and the most profound and far-reaching changes, have really turned upon religious questions; and that the stronger and more definite has been the religion, the more fundamental and striking have been these results. Thus, for instance, the modern history of Europe has been little else than a

[1] Froude: Hist. Engl. xii. 535.

history of struggles fundamentally religious. A recent historian of civilisation has indeed maintained that this is true only of the past,[1] and that the present age has more and more learned to restrict its enthusiasm to material objects. But he forgets that religion does not cease to influence events among those who reject its claims: it excites the strongest human passions not merely in its defenders, but in its enemies. The claim to hold communion with an unseen world irritates when it does not win and satisfy. Atheism has again and again been a fanaticism; it has been a missionary and a persecutor by turns; it is lashed into passion by the very presence of the sublime passion to which it is opposed. We of to-day know full well that no political subjects are discussed so warmly as those which bear even remotely upon religion. "The deepest subject," says Goethe, "in the history of the world and of mankind, and that to which all others are subordinate, is the conflict between faith and unbelief."[2]

While these causes make an interest in religion, of whatever kind, inevitable among thoughtful men in our day and generation, they only reinforce, they do not obscure or supersede, those permanent reasons for its influence, which are part of our natural and human circumstances. Among these it may suffice to mention one. It is a fact, certain to each one of us, that we shall individually die. If science could arrest the empire of death, as it has limited that of disease; if thought, in its onward march throughout the centuries, could rob us utterly of the presentiment of an im-

[1] Buckle: Hist. Civ. i. 241-325. [2] Qu. by Luthardt.

mortality and of our aspirations towards a higher world, then religion would retain, in the fixed circumstances of life, no ally of anything like equal power. But there is the certainty, present to each one of us in our thoughtful moments, never entirely absent from the thought of those who seriously think at all, that an hour will come when we shall face the problem of problems for ourselves and alone; when we shall know by experience what really is beyond the veil, and how it is related to that which we see and are here; and it is impossible, with this prospect before us, to treat the voice and claims of religion as wholly trivial or unimportant.[1]

But here the question arises as to what it is that man seeks in seeking religion. Or rather, what is religion? We know it when we meet it in life; we know it by its bearing, by its fruits, by the atmosphere with which it surrounds itself. But what is it within the soul? what is its chief element or substance? What is this power which does not meet the eye, but which we trace in its results? what is the true psychological account that must be given of it?

I.

As we repeat the question, "What is religion," we find ourselves, it may be, in the position of standing face to face

[1] This is admitted, although, of course, in terms which the writer would not adopt, by Mr. Buckle. Hist. Civ. i. 113.

with a very old acquaintance, with whose countenance and habits we have been familiar all our lives, but of whose real self we cannot but feel we have a somewhat shadowy perception.

1. Is religion, then, in the heart of man, to be looked upon chiefly as the highest and purest form of feeling? Is feeling the essential thing in true religion? So thought no less a person than Schleiermacher.[1] He makes religion to consist in feeling—notably in our feeling of dependence on a Higher Power; and his influence has won for this representation a wide acceptance in modern Protestant Germany.[2] Such in England is, or has been at times, the practical instinct, if not the decision, of Wesleyanism and kindred systems.[3] Feeling, not knowledge; feeling, not morality; feeling, not even conscience, is the test of acceptance—that is to say, of satisfactory religion. Acceptance is warranted by the sense of acceptance; religious progress is measured by the sense of enjoying more and more the raptures of the religious life.

Nor, if we look either into the recesses of the human heart, or into the historical expressions of religious earnest-

[1] Schleiermacher, Christliche Glaube, i. pp. 6-14. He is expanding the proposition that "Die Frömmigkeit, welche die Basis aller kirchlichen Gemeinschaften ausmacht, ist rein für sich betrachtet weder ein Wissen noch ein Thun, sondern ein Bestimmtheit des Gefühls oder des unmittelbaren Selbstbewusstseins." Compare p. 16. Das gemeinsame aller derjenigen Bestimmtheiten des Selbstbewusstseins, welche überwiegend ein Irgendwohergetroffensein der Empfänglichkeit aussagen, ist dass wir uns als abhängig fühlen.

[2] As with Nitzsch, Twesten, and others. Cf. Grimm, Inst. Th. Dogm. p. 19.

[3] Compare the remarks in Southey's "Life of Wesley," p. 267.

ness, can the high place of feeling in the religious life be rightly depreciated. Feeling is the play of our consciousness coming into contact with its object: it varies in intensity according to the interest we take in that object: it is a totally different thing in the case of a casual acquaintance and of a near relative. When, then, the soul is in intimate contact with the Object of objects—with God,—feeling, the purest and the most intense, is not merely legitimate, but ordinarily inevitable. How much of the Psalter is feeling—the tenderest, the strongest, the most loyal, the most affectionate! "Like as the hart desireth the water-brooks, so longeth my soul after Thee, O God. My soul is athirst for God, yea, even for the living God: when shall I come to appear before the presence of God?" "Whom have I in heaven but Thee, and there is none upon earth that I desire in comparison of Thee!" "My soul hangeth upon Thee: Thy right hand hath upholden me." "Do not I hate them, O Lord, that hate Thee, and am not I grieved with those that rise up against Thee: yea, I hate them right sore, even as though they were mine enemies!"[1] How profoundly is the religion of S. Paul, as we study it in his Epistles, penetrated by feeling! Always in felt contact with an unseen Master; he is tender, he is vehement, he burns, he is melted: his dispositions towards his fellow-men are so various and keen, because in him feeling has been educated in a higher Presence.—"The love of Christ constraineth us:" "To me to live is Christ:" "Who

[1] Ps. xlii. 1; lxxiii. 25; lxiii. 8; cxxxix. 21-22.

shall separate us from the love of Christ?" "I live; yet not I, but Christ liveth in me:" "If any man love not the Lord Jesus Christ, let him be anathema maranatha."[1]

But the question is not whether feeling be an element of sincere religion; but whether it be the one most essential element. And here two observations cannot fail to strike us.

In the long run, there can be, for well-ordered minds, no strong play of feeling apart from a sense of the intellectual truth of the object upon which feeling is bestowed. To lavish feeling, if it be possible to do so, upon a personage who is even suspected of being mythical or half mythical, is to prostitute feeling. Some idea, then, of the object of feeling must precede the feeling, as well as a conviction of the truth of the object so conceived of. We are told that religious feeling is especially the sense of entire dependence upon a Higher Power: man's inmost soul hangs confidingly upon the Power in which we live and move and have our being. But, then, what is this power? That is a question which must be answered before feeling can determine its complexion. Is this power an impersonal force? is it a blind fate or destiny? is it some vast machine, having neither heart nor will, but moving onwards through endless cycles of destructions and recombinations, of life and death, unceasingly, resistlessly, inexorably? If so, feeling at least cannot take the form of absolute dependence: there is no such thing as surrendering yourself in trustful resignation to a piece of machinery,

[1] 2 Cor. v. 14; Phil. i. 21; Rom. viii. 35; Gal. ii. 20; 1 Cor xvi. 22.

which may crush you to death at any moment in its advance. Trustful dependence is only possible when that on which we depend is seen to be a Person, and a *moral* Person, that is to say, holy, truthful, compassionate, just. But here we pass out of the region of feeling. It appears that before feeling can trust itself, something is wanted to guide and colour it. Knowledge is at least as essential to religion as feeling; and knowledge of the Object of religion, expressed in clear and precise terms, is after all only another name for dogma.

But, moreover, feeling, even if intelligent, must accompany right moral effort, in order to be religious. Feeling, even when directed to heavenly objects, may be, in its substance, partly physical; and there is no necessary connection between feeling so originating and moral earnestness, or even a right morality. Nay, it is very possible for those who feel warmly to imagine, mistakenly enough, that warm feeling is the same thing as, or an adequate substitute for, acting rightly. He who said, "If ye love Me, keep My commandments,"[1] implied that there are forms of religious passion, distinct no doubt from the true Christian grace of love, which may co-exist with disobedience, and may even appear to compensate for it. The Galatians had not been the less willing to "pluck out their own eyes," out of devotion to S. Paul, at the time of their conversion, because they afterwards looked on him as a personal enemy for telling them the truth about the Judaisers.[2] The

[1] S. John xiv. 15. [2] Gal. iv. 15, 16.

Apostle was not insincere who protested, "Though I should die with Thee, yet will I not deny Thee;"[1] albeit a few hours later, at the crisis of danger, he could exclaim, "I know not the Man."[2] Feeling is not necessarily moral purpose; and its possible deficiencies on this side, as well as on the side of knowledge, shew that we cannot regard it as alone forming the raw material of religious life.[3]

2. Is it then more nearly true to say that the one essential thing in religion is knowledge—knowledge of God and of the things of God? Somewhat of this kind was the opinion of the Gnostics of the second century. They regarded the Christian doctrines as simply an addition to the existing stock of current human speculations, and they ventilated what appear to us nothing less than the wildest fancies under the protection of current Christian phrases, which served to decorate and recommend speculations that often had nothing to do with Christianity. They thought that the Apostles had been unintellectual persons, upon whose well-meant efforts they had themselves improved.[4] Since faith has in it a large moral element, their watchword was, not *faith*, but *knowledge;* and,

[1] S. Matt. xxvi. 35. [2] S. Matt. xxvi. 72, 74.

[3] Hegel, Werke, xvii. 295 (qu. Grimm). Gründet sich die Religion im Menschen nur auf ein Gefühl, so hat solches richtig keine weitere Bestimmung als das Gefühl seiner Abhängigkeit zu seyn, und so wäre der Hund der beste Christ, denn er trägt dieses am stärksten in sich, und lebt vornehmlich in diesem Gefühle. Auch erlosungsgefühle hat der Hund, wenn seinem Hunger durch einen Knochen Befriedigung wird." This does not exclude the truth that the affectionate loyalty of a dog for his master is a rebuke to the coldheartedness of Christians; but it is rightly implied that the religion of humanity must be based on something more than feeling.

[4] S. Irenæus, Hær. III. 12, 12.

in their own phrase, this knowledge was to be the salvation of souls.[1]

The history of the human mind repeats itself, and a position which is at bottom akin to the foregoing, is familiar to some of us in the philosophies of Schelling and Hegel. Here too faith is only the lower grade, the popular form of the religious consciousness; its most cherished doctrines are only parables of the realities open to the eye of science upon which the modern thinker may gaze. His religion is thus mainly an effort of the intellect, which is perpetually engaged in disentangling and distilling from the rude forms of old-world creeds those abstract scientific conceptions which are better suited to the palate of modern philosophy.[2]

It has already been implied that knowledge—true knowledge of truth—is of vital importance to religion. No one would question this, except in the interests of a morbid fanaticism. Religion is impossible without some knowledge of its object; and our capacities for true religious life must, to a certain extent, vary with our varying degrees of religious knowledge.[3] "This," says our Saviour, "is

[1] Compare the account which S. Irenæus gives of the Valentinians, Hær. i. 6, 2. Their contemptuous estimate of Catholic Christians is expressed in the phrase "*οἱ δὶ ἔργων καὶ πίστεως ψιλῆς βεβαιούμενοι καὶ μὴ τὴν τελείαν γνῶσιν ἔχοντες.*"

[2] In the words of a more recent Hegelian writer, "Dass der Inhalt der Religion und Philosophie derselbe sey, indem den Vorstellungen des religiösen Bewusstseyns ein ihner fern liegender Sinn untergelegt wird, den man unverholen auszusprechen sich nicht getrauen darf. *Daumer, Andeutung eines Systemes speculativer Philosophie*, p. 45, qu. by Grimm.

[3] Rom. x. 2; Eph. i. 17; iv. 13; Phil. i. 9; Col. . 9, 10; ii . 2; 1 Tim. ii. 4; 2 Tim. iii. 7; Heb. x. 26; 2 Pet. i. 2, 3, 8; ii. 20.

life eternal; that they may know Thee, the only true God, and Jesus Christ, Whom Thou hast sent."[1] The knowledge spoken of here, and elsewhere in the Bible, is indeed not merely intellectual: it is knowledge in act; it is the knowledge which is won by love and obedience, as distinct from, although together with, intelligence. Nevertheless, knowledge, in its ordinary sense of information apprehended by the understanding, is indispensable to religion. Sight is not the power of walking or working; but we cannot work or walk blindfolded without disaster.

Yet no mere action of the intelligence, however active, upon the subject-matter of religion, is the true back-bone of religion. Knowledge alone may only enhance responsibility. If Christ had not come and spoken to the Jews, they had not had sin: as it was, they had no cloke for their sin.[2] S. Paul contrasts a merely intelligent apprehension of religious subjects with love. "Knowledge," he says, "puffeth up, but charity edifieth."[3] The whole drift of S. James' Epistle goes to shew the worthlessness, religiously speaking, of unfruitful knowledge. The hearer of the Word who is not a doer, is compared with the man who continueth in the perfect law of liberty besides looking into it. The first does but realize a fleeting and unproductive impression; the second has undergone a change of life.[4]

The most intellectual of the Greeks, whose thoughts about God and the soul might at times almost seem to anticipate

[1] S. John xvii. 3.
[2] S. John xv. 22; ix. 41.
[3] 1 Cor. viii. 1.
[4] S. James i. 22-24.

Christianity, as they have been welcomed with the respect of many a generation of Christians, has unwittingly warned us of the religious impotence of mere culture, by staining his pages, not once or twice, but habitually, with sympathetic references to crimes, tolerable enough to the public sentiment of Athens, but the very names of which are defiling to Christian lips. The most intellectual Gnostics were sensualists; sensualists upon a theory and with deliberation.[1] And modern history, if it were worth our while to consult it here, yields many a warning that intellectual culture about religious things is one thing, and genuine religion quite another. Henry VIII., who had been destined for the English Primacy, was among the best read theologians of his day; but whatever opinion may be entertained of his place, as a far-sighted statesman, in English history, no one would seriously speak of him as personally religious.

Intelligence indeed, however cultivated, is only a department of human life. Man is something greater than a cultivated intellect; even than an intellect cultivated by study of the highest objects that can be presented to it,—by study of the things of God. More than this is needed to constitute religion; which, if it be not merely a sentiment or passion, so certainly it is more than an intellectual effort, however serious be its purpose or sublime its goal.

3. Are we then to say, with a large section of the modern world, that the essential thing in religion is morality? This

[1] S. Irenæus, Hær. i. 6, 3. *διὸ δὴ καὶ τὰ ἀπειργμένα πάντα ἀδεῶς οἱ τελειότατοι πράττουσιν αὐτῶν, περὶ ὧν αἱ γραφαὶ διαβεβαιοῦνται, τοὺς ποιοῦντας αὐτὰ βασιλείαν Θεοῦ μὴ κληρονομήσειν.* Cf. 1 Cor. vi. 9, 10.

was the teaching of Immanuel Kant. Religion, as he phrases it, is a practical recognition of the Divine origin of the moral law.[1] And it is a doctrine which constantly meets us in the society and the general literature of our own country at the present day. Its popularity is easy of explanation in an age when belief in the Unseen has been seriously weakened among those classes of the people to which the political necessity of strengthening virtues which purify life and uphold society is pre-eminently obvious.

And certainly we must admit that religion has no more appropriate work than the regulation of human life in accordance with moral truth: it is in this province especially that we look for evidences of its reality and its power. "By their fruits ye shall know them,"[2] said its one great Master, of certain religious aspirants. "Pure religion," according to His Apostle, "and undefiled before God and the Father, is this, to visit the fatherless and widows in their affliction, and to keep himself unspotted from the world."[3] In other words, it is active philanthropy and personal purity. The language used to describe it in the Bible, implies that knowledge of religion and religious emotion are, as we have seen, worse than incomplete, if they do not lead to active goodness.[4] What a man knows or feels is of little import, until it is ascertained what he does, or rather what he is.[5]

But it by no means follows that morality can be truly described as the essence of religion. It differs from religion

[1] Quot. in Luthardt: Apologetische Vorträge, l. 6. [2] S. Matt. vii. 16.
[3] S. James i. 27. [4] S. Matt. vii. 22, 23; 2 S. Pet. ii. 20, 21.
[5] Ps. xv. i. *sqq.*; xxiv. 3, 5; Rom. viii. 13, 14.

in this, that morality is conformity to a law of right, while religion is essentially a relation towards a Person. A perfect, absolute morality will cover the same practical ground as true religion. But if men endeavour to treat morality as the only essential element in religion, and accordingly attempt to plant it on some independent basis, physical or otherwise, of its own—two things will happen. Such a morality will be much narrower than a religious morality; it will, in the judgment of religious men, present an incomplete view of the real cycle of duty; notably, it will fail to recognize that most important side of duty which we owe exclusively to God. But, besides this, morality, divorced from religion, will tend more and more, from the nature of the case, to approximate to a department of mere human law; to concern itself only with acts and not with motives; to make the external product, and not the internal governing principle, the supreme consideration. Morality, severed from religious motive, is like a branch cut off from a tree: it may, here and there, from accidental causes, retain its greenness for a while; but its chance of vigorous life is a very slender one. Nor is it possible to popularize a real morality, a morality that shall deal with motives as well as with acts, without unveiling to the eye of the soul something more personal than an abstract law. It is when man has caught sight of the one Perfect Being, and in the effort to escape from the weakness and degradations of his own earthly life, "lifts up his soul" to this unseen, all-powerful, all-bountiful Friend, that he may hope to discover the true ideal of his life, and to realize it. Religion is thus the constant spring and best guarantee of morality; but morality is not the "essence of religion." Religion consists fundamentally in the practical recognition of a constraining bond between the inward life of man and an unseen Person.[1]

The ancients were fond of discussing the derivation of the word religion; and Cicero refers it to that anxious habit of mind which cons over again and again all that bears on the service of heaven.[2] Lactantius may be wrong in his etymology, but he has certainly seized the broad popular sense of the word, when he connects it with the idea of an obligation by which man is bound to an invisible Lord.[3]

With this the Biblical phraseology is in substantial harmony. The expressions which describe the religion of the earliest Patriarchs are in point; and, like much else in the Pentateuch, they mould the later language of the Psalter. Enoch and Noah are said to have "walked with God;" Abraham was bidden "walk before the face of God, and be perfect."[4] Here God is represented as the bounden Companion of a man's life, as well as his all-surveying Judge and Master; and this idea of religion as personal devotedness to God underlies all the representations of Scripture

[1] Compare Eus. Præp. Ev. 1, 2. *ἡ πρὸς τὸν ἕνα καὶ μόνον ὡς ἀληθῶς ὁμολογουμενόν τε καὶ ὄντα Θεὸν ἀνάνευσις καὶ ἡ κατὰ τοῦτον ζωή.*

[2] Nat. Deor. ii. 28. Qui omnia quæ ad cultum deorum pertinerent, diligenter retractarent et tanquam relegerent, religiosi dicti sunt ex relegendo.

[3] Inst. Div. iv. 28. Vinculo pietatis obstricti, Deo religati sumus, unde ipsa religio nomen cepit. Compare the hostile phrase of Lucretius, "religionum se nodis solvere." Cf. St. Aug. Retract. 1. 13; de verâ relig. xli. 55.

[4] Gen. v. 24; vi. 9; xvii. 1.

on the subject. Religion in the understanding, is the knowledge of God,[1]—of His will and commandments; it is the knowledge of His "mystery" or secret counsel revealed in Christ.[2] When the Jewish law had been given, religion was practically a "walking in the law of the Lord;"[3] when the Christian revelation has been made, it is an "acknowledgment of the truth which is after godliness."[4] But in this truth, in that law, it seeks a Person; it is fundamentally the maintenance of a real relation with the Personal God, or with a Divine Person really incarnate in Jesus Christ. Accordingly, religion, both Jewish and Christian, is described as a covenant; it is a bond or understanding between the nation or the soul and God; or, still more, from the point of view of a faith that worketh by love, it is personal communion with God. "That which we have seen and heard," says S. John, "declare we unto you, that ye also may have communion with us, and truly our communion is with the Father, and with His Son Jesus Christ."[5]

Thus religious life is more than feeling, since feeling may be physical, misdirected, selfish. It is more than knowledge, which, even if it be complete and accurate, may fail to govern the moral nature. It is more than obedience to a moral code, because such obedience, if sufficiently complete to be religious, already implies relations to the Lawgiver. And yet religion is feeling; it is mental illumination; it is especially moral effort; because it is that which implies, and comprehends, and combines them all. It is the sacred

[1] Hos. iv. 1. [2] Eph. i. 17.
[3] Ps. cxix. 1; Cf. S. Luke i. 6. [4] Tit. i. 1. [5] 1 S. John i. 3.

bond, freely accepted, generously, enthusiastically, persistently welcomed, whereby the soul engages to make a continuous expenditure of its highest powers in attaching itself to the Personal Source and Object of its being. It is the tie by which the soul binds itself to God, its true friend. To be thus bound to a person is to cherish strong, nay, passionate feelings towards him; it is to seek to know all that can be known about his wishes and character, and to register this knowledge in exact terms; it is to obey scrupulously all that is clearly ascertained to be his will. "Shew Thou me the way that I should walk in, for I lift up my soul unto Thee." This is the language of feeling, pure and strong; it is the language of intelligence, ever desiring a higher knowledge of its Highest Object; it is the language of obedience, the most absolute that man can proffer. It is these, because it is the voice, the exceeding great cry, of that unquenchable passion, of that irrepressible aspiration, whereby the soul of man shews forth its truest dignity and highest virtue in seeking the better to know and love and serve its Highest and Invisible Object; because, in a word, it is the language of religion.

II.

If the prayer of the human soul be granted, can we infer from the needs of the suppliant any of the necessary characteristics of the great gift which is to relieve them? To say that we can do so will not be "dictating terms to God," because He is not more the author of a religious Revelation than of the moral and mental instincts which demand it. To say that we can do so will not involve our "paying court to the corrupt instincts of a fallen nature;" because it certainly is not these instincts which seek a close approach to a nearer vision of the Throne of Moral Purity and Light. Nor will it compromise the True Faith by drawing attention to some features which are, and must be, more or less common to it with the false faiths whereby man, again and again, during his long and weary history, has sought to satisfy the noblest of his passions, even when he has only lighted up the dark canopy of heaven from fires kindled by himself on earth. For in order to exist at all, false beliefs must embody some, even considerable elements of truth; and conversely, the True Faith, in order to be itself, must have something, both in its form and in its substance, common to itself and to every falsehood that opposes it.

1. First of all, then, an answer from God to the religious needs of man will be, at least in some degree, a mysterious answer: it will half unveil much which shades off into the unknown and the incomprehensible. To profess to reveal the Infinite, and yet to undertake to explain everything to the perfect satisfaction of a finite understanding, is worse than unreasonable. And a creed which should discover nothing that lies beyond the province of our experience, can

have no pretensions to be a religious creed at all. For religion is not a relation to or communion with nature, or with any natural force or law; it is communion with an Invisible Person. Certainly, we hear men speak of a religion of art, of a religion of work, of a religion of civilisation. Harmless metaphors these, if it be only meant that all the occupations of life can and should be penetrated and sanctified by the sense of God's Presence and Will; but mischievous and misleading to the last degree, if it be suggested that either art, or work, or civilisation is in itself an end worthy of the highest energies of the human spirit. He only who made us for Himself—the Infinite and Eternal God—can be the object of religion, and any serious answer to the religious aspirations of humanity must point to *Him*. "Our preachers," said a German writer, referring to his university some thirty years ago, "having got rid of the Christian doctrines by means of the higher criticism, are now insisting with much earnestness upon the importance of taking regular exercise." [1] Regular exercise is no doubt a matter of real importance in its way: but an advocacy of its advantages, however impassioned, says nothing to that side of our being which breathes the prayer, "Shew Thou me the way that I should walk in, for I lift up my soul unto Thee."

That Christianity is mysterious, is no new objection against it. Unquestionably it is mysterious. In the year 1702, Toland undertook to prove that "Christianity is not mysterious:" but he only succeeded in leading a certain num-

[1] Dr. Tholuck to Dr. Pusey.

ber of minds to a belief that it is false. That "the Gospel contains nothing contrary to reason" is the conviction of every Christian, who knows that right reason and revelation are alike gifts of God. That the Gospel "contains nothing above reason," is an assertion so paradoxical, as to be undeserving of a reply from those who believe that the historical and doctrinal statements of the New Testament are integral elements of the Gospel. Toland, indeed, could only make any approach to demonstrating his thesis, by tampering with the ordinary and world-wide sense of the term "Mystery;" and since the days of Toland science herself has, by her discoveries, made men feel more keenly than did our fathers the mysteriousness of Nature, and through Nature, of Nature's GOD.

2. Next, God's answer to man's prayer must, at least within limits, be definite. An answer made up altogether of vague hopes, aspirations, surmisings, guesses, probabilities, whatever its other merits, will not meet the specific needs of man. What does man seek in seeking a religious creed? He seeks intellectual satisfaction and moral support. His intellect asks for reliable information upon certain subjects of the most momentous importance. How does he come to be here? Whither is he going? What is the purpose and drift of the various forms of existence around him? Above all, what is the nature, what are the attributes and dispositions, of that Being to Whom the highest yearnings of his inmost self constantly point as the true object of his existence? In asking that the answers to these questions shall be

definite, that what is certain shall be affirmed as certain, what is doubtful as doubtful, what is false as false, he is only asking that his religious information shall be presented in as clear and practical a shape as his information on other subjects. In no department of human knowledge is haziness deemed a merit: by nothing is an educated mind more distinguished than by the resolute effort to mark the exact frontiers of its knowledge and its ignorance; to hesitate only when hesitation is necessary; to despair of knowledge only when knowledge is ascertainably out of reach. Surely on the highest and most momentous of all subjects this same precision may be asked for with reverence and in reason; surely the human mind is not bound to forget its noblest instincts when it approaches the throne and presence of its Maker.

Yet more necessary are definite statements of truth and duty to the moral side of human life. To obey at all, we must know what are the true limits of obedience, and what the nature and authority of the lawgiver. A soldier under fire has two things to do: first to attend to the word of his commanding officer, and then to strengthen his will by all the considerations which may enable him to do his duty. Man, as a moral being, is engaged in a perpetual campaign against the invading forces of temptation which assail him from without, and the insurrectionary outbreaks of lawless passions from within. If he is to make a successful resistance, he must be penetrated by a conviction that it is of vital importance to resist to the last extremity. This conviction must itself be made up of and depend upon other convictions, such as the sanctity of God, His power, His omnipresence, the interest which He takes in our success, the strength with which He supplies us, the certainty that He will come to judge us. A faltering, hazy representation may feed an aimless sentimentalism; it is useless for the purposes of an earnest moral struggle.

An exact creed and code of conduct is therefore a need of man's mental and moral nature, and all religious systems, whatever their truth or falsehood, have attempted to satisfy it. The answer to this need, with which we are familiar, is that contained in the Christian theology; and we use that word in its broad sense, as including the whole cycle of revealed doctrine and morals. Theology, in its scientific exhibition, results from the effort which the Christian mind makes from age to age to reduce to a precise and working form the deposit of truth committed at the first to the Christian Church. It is the elaborate inventory which century after century the Church has been taking of the priceless treasures which were committed to her keeping in the age of the Apostles. What doctrines may and may not be catalogued in that inventory without serious inaccuracy, is a point upon which, unhappily, there are wide divisions in the Christian world; but in the fifty generations of Christians from the first until the present age there has never been any sort of question as to the duty of ascertaining, as correctly as may be, what are the truths which Christ and His Apostles have taught, what is the exact area and import of these truths, what their moral and social significance, what our practical duties towards them.

Yes; but it is said, has not this inveterate instinct of the Christian mind been fatal to the beauty of religious truth? Is not religious truth better left in the vague, hazy distance of popular thought? Is it not vulgarized by this nearer probing, by this inquisitive anxiety to make out exactly what it is? Is not the New Testament vague and undecided, and are we likely to improve upon it? Are not the clergy, too, under a temptation to confuse between their professional instinct of making the most of their title-deeds, and the real broad interests of Christendom? Has not Christendom, in fact, suffered by over-definitions, by false definitions; and this in former ages as certainly as in our own?

Certainly there are arguments which may be urged against definitions; and first of all on æsthetic grounds. A picture of Turner's is a more beautiful thing than a working drawing; but if your object be to give the measurements of a public edifice, Turner's picture would not be the more useful guide of the two. It is easy to advise a man to "study and admire the poetry of Isaiah and S. John, without troubling himself with the truth of their theological dogmas, or even of their historical statements." No doubt the poetry of the Evangelist and of the Prophet is of consummate beauty, but it is not their poetry which has impressed them on the thought and heart of the Christian world. The really important question about both these writers is, what do they exactly teach upon the gravest subjects that can interest thoughtful men? And next, is their teaching true? The answer to this, to be worth having, must be a sharply defined answer; and art, if needs be, must make a sacrifice to the demands of truth. That there have been unnecessary definitions, rash definitions, false definitions in Christendom, must be frankly granted; that they are still possible cannot be denied, in view of contemporary events; that they have injured the cause of Christ cannot be doubted. But the question is as to the principle of definiteness, not as to its abuse: false definitions, like false miracles, imply the true, of which they are a counterfeit and caricature. As to the New Testament, those who speak of its teaching as indefinite, appear to confuse between its substance and its form. Made up as it is of four biographical sketches, of one narrative of the lives and works of some missionary teachers, of twenty-one letters, six of them addressed to individuals, and of one description of a heavenly vision, its form is, of necessity, unmethodical; it is, if you will, anti-scholastic. But its form is distinct from its substance; and from age to age the clear import of its substance is pressed upon the imagination and heart of the world by the matchless beauties of its form. The teaching of the New Testament indefinite! It is simple paradox. What can be more definite than the account of Christ's Birth, of His Miracles, of His Resurrection, of His Ascension into heaven, in the first three Gospels? What more definite than the awful representation of His Person in the fourth?

Is the account of justification in the Epistle to the Romans and the Galatians indefinite? Or that of the Eucharist and the supernatural gifts of the Spirit in the First Epistle to the Corinthians, or that of the incorporation of the Church with the living and triumphant Christ in the letters to the Colossians and Ephesians, or that of its organization in the Pastoral Epistles? Is it not rather true that the New Testament is much too definite for modern unbelief, and that the real crime of the Church is, not that she has added the quality of definiteness to the writings of the Apostles and the Evangelists, but that she has persistently called attention to that quality which from the first, and from the nature of the case, belonged to them?

How, indeed, could it be otherwise? How would the cry of humanity for light and guidance have been answered? how would it not rather have been mocked and scorned, by a revelation of the indefinite; by a revelation of mists whereof none could decide the frontiers, or unfold the meaning, or insist upon the worth? Such a revelation would have in fact revealed nothing; nothing that might not have been in some degree surmised by reason; nothing that could invigorate the heart or control the will. And in Christianity God has not disappointed us. He has not contrived to say much without asserting anything. If our Heavenly Father has not answered the petition of His children for the solid bread of truth with a stone, He as certainly has not met it with a transcendental vapour.

3. Thirdly, a real answer to the religious needs of man must be positive. It must state what is truth, and not merely what is not truth. The soul of man does not look inward and upward only in the hope of detecting falsehoods: its deepest desire is to know, not what is not, but what is. Merely negative teachers are as the wind; they destroy but they cannot build; at their best they do but sweep away the unsubstantial fictions of human fancy or human fraud, but they erect nothing solid in the place of the discarded fictions. Positive truth alone can feed, sustain, invigorate the soul. It is no support in the hour of despondency or in the hour of temptation to reflect or to be told that such and such a doctrine or system is false. Possibly enough it *is* false; but what then? Does a sense of its falsehood nerve the will to do and the heart to sustain when action and endurance are hard? A sense of falsehood only supplies moral power so long and so far as you are confronted with the falsehood. You hate the lie, and your hatred imports force into your contradiction; you loathe the idol, and a righteous scorn nerves your arm to shatter it. But when the idol has been pulverized and the lie is exploded, your force is gone. Your force was purely relative to the objects of its animosity, and it perished with them. Nay, more; even while they lasted, your force was good for nothing beyond and beside the function of destroying them. Such force is like Jehu; it is trenchant energy so long as vengeance has to be wreaked upon the house of Ahab; but it is abject impotence when the time comes for settling the polity of Israel on a sure foundation, and of

storing up a legacy of strength and safety for the coming times. Positive doctrine, on the other hand is, or ought to be, moral power. The whisper in the heart of the moral fool, "there is no God," can never add to his stock of moral strength. The faith of the Psalmist, "the Lord liveth," is at once followed by the exclamation, "and blessed be my strong Helper, and praised be the God of my salvation."[1] The soul cannot rest upon the void which is the result of that vast negation: it can and does draw comfort, strength, support, determination, as it grasps and leans upon this greatest of all assertions.

This is a point which requires insisting on, especially in an age of criticism. Here and there criticism may vindicate an affirmation; its more ordinary occupation is to destroy. It almost proceeds upon the assumption that the soil of truth is encumbered on all sides with brushwood and rubbish, and that it can scarcely do wrong in burning and clearing away for ever. We may allow that there is legitimate and useful work for it to do; but it is not the less true that the temper of mind which it creates is prone to entertain a most serious misapprehension on religious matters. It tends to beget the notion that religious truth is simply negation—negation of false beliefs, negation of superstitious practices, negation of the errors and mistakes of other people; but scarcely anything that is really positive, with a body and substance of its own. Very many people in this country, especially among the educated

[1] Ps. xviii. 47.

classes, conceive of religion in this way, and to their own unspeakable loss. What God is not, what Christ is not, what the atonement and work of Christ are not, what prayer is not, what sacraments are not;—these are the questions with which they concern themselves almost exclusively. Yet the only question that is lastingly practical is what God, Christ, the atonement, prayer, the sacraments *are.* The negative conclusion does nothing beyond removing one or more misconceptions, or being supposed to do so; or rather it does something which were better undone. It satisfies the vague sense that religion is too important a concern to be entirely passed by: it furnishes a form of interest in religion, of strictly intellectual interest, that may be warranted to entail no practical consequences. And thus the half-awakened conscience is again lulled to sleep, by encountering a religious idea which only presents itself to be discarded; and the eyes of the spirit close, perhaps for ever.

Do I say that a true faith has no negative aspects? Certainly not. The Jewish faith was a negation of Polytheism: Christianity is a negation of Polytheism, and of much besides. The most characteristic writings of the great Apostle are protests against false ideas of the work of Christ: the most elaborate of the Catholic creeds contains a repudiation of errors which deny the truth of the Divine Nature, or the truth of the Person of Jesus. But in these cases the negation does not stand alone; it is only the inevitable corollary of a greater affirmation. Unlike the dreary criticism which makes a solitude in the human spirit, and then sardonically calls it peace, the negations of the Creed do but remove obstructions to its positive statements: they clear a space in thought for laying the foundations and raising the walls of a solid edifice, within which the Divine Architect has provided for the most urgent wants of man.

4. Yet again, if man's deepest needs are to be satisfied, he must believe that his creed is absolutely, and not merely relatively, true. Relative truth—truth which is true only to certain persons or under certain circumstances—ceases to be truth when those persons and circumstances pass. It is transient; and to say that truth is transient, is to qualify the idea of truth by an attribute which destroys it. Relative truth is not truth, in the plain sense of the term; it is only opinion; it is opinion which in the event proves to be unfounded.

We are often told that Christianity, like the other positive religions of the world, is relatively true; and hard words are used of Christians, who say that its truth is absolute if it be true at all. Yet how can a creed profess to be relatively true without admitting itself to be really false? It was pardonable in Benhadad's Syrians to suggest that the God of Israel was only a God of the hills; but no believing Israelite could have granted this without denying the first article of his creed. And Philosophy has sometimes meant to befriend Christianity, by asserting that it teaches a relative truth. She bids believers make the best of it, on the ground that if not absolutely true, it is a phase of truth, true to the believer, true provisionally, although liable to be superseded by a higher truth in days to come. But who could make the most of a creed with such an estimate of its worth as this? Would any sensible man die for a "relatively true" religion? Could it teach him the duties of prayer or self-sacrifice? Would he live for it? Would he be even interested for long in a philosophy which he believed to be only relatively true? While the Ptolemaic system of the heavens lasted, it was supposed to be absolutely true: Would the ancient world have listened quietly to the Ptolemaic teachers had it suspected, however distantly, the advent of a Copernicus? The ceremonial element in the Jewish dispensation, as S. Paul has taught us, was only of relative authority. But it was believed by the Jews to be absolute. To see in it "a figure of the time then present," was already to have become a Christian. Any creed, whether true or false, must claim to be absolute, or it must make no claim at all, since upon faith in its absolute truth depends the necessity and reasonableness of all the acts, habits, efforts, sacrifices, which constitute its practical side—all the ventures, in short, which men make on account of it.

To say that Christianity is only relatively true; that it is but the prelude and introduction to some broader religion of humanity, which will in time supersede it, is, in fact, to reject Christianity. For from the first Christianity has claimed to be the Universal Religion. It was destined from the first to embrace the whole world; it was to last throughout the ages. "Go ye," said its Founder, "and make disciples of all nations, baptizing them in the name of the Father, and of the Son, and of the Holy Ghost;" and, "lo, I am with you alway, even unto the end of the world."[1] In this claim of universality, whether in time or range of empire, there lay the implied and further claim to be the Absolute Religion—the one final unveiling of the Universal Father's mind before the eyes of His children.[2] This conviction underlies S. Paul's earnest apostolate of the Gentiles in the face of active Jewish prejudice. He "owed"[3] the absolute religion, as he could have owed no relative religion whatever, to the Greeks and to the Barbarians alike, to the philosophers and to the uneducated. To his eye all the deepest divisions of country, race, and station vanished entirely as men passed within the Church. "There is," he exclaimed, "neither Greek nor Jew, circumcision nor uncircumcision, Barbarian, Scythian, bond nor free, but Christ is all, and in all."[4] A religion conscious of being suitable only to particular dates or localities could never have originally aspired to bring within the range of its influence all the varieties of race and thought that are found in the human family. It would feel its unsuitableness to some races, to some civilizations, to some historical periods, if not to all. "To make all men see what is the fellowship of the mystery which from the beginning of the world hath been

[1] S. Matt. xxviii. 19, 20.

[2] Baur: Vorlesungen über Neutestamentliche Theologie, p. 131.

[3] Rom. i. 14.

[4] Col. iii. 11; cf. Gal. iii. 28.

hid in God,"[1] was an ambition appropriate "to the faith once for all delivered to the Saints."[2]

5. Lastly, if man's religious wants are to be answered, his creed must speak, not merely to his intelligence, but to his heart and will. He cannot really rest upon the most unimpeachable abstractions. He needs something warmer than the truest philosophy. He yearns to come in contact with a heart; and no religion therefore can really satisfy him which does not at least lead him to know and love a person. An unseen Friend, who will purify, and teach, and check, and lead, and sustain him:—that is his great necessity. And this want, this last but deepest want of man's religious life, Christianity has satisfied. As humanity, "sitting in darkness and in the shadow of death," pleads with the Power Whom it feels but cannot see—"Shew Thou me the way that I should walk in, for I lift up my soul unto Thee"—lo! the heavens drop down from above, and the skies pour forth righteousness. And One fairer than the children of men presents Himself to all the centuries and countries of the world with the gracious bidding, "Come unto Me, all ye that labour and are heavy laden, and I will give you rest."[3]

In the Lectures which are to follow during the succeeding Sundays of Lent, an attempt will be made to insist upon some of the truths which are most fundamentally related to the soul's religious life, as they come into contact with some forms of modern thought. Of so vast a subject a few fragments are all that, from the nature of the case,

[1] Eph. iii. 9. [2] S. Jude 3. [3] S. Matt. xi. 28.

can possibly be offered. If we could say all that could be said, such truths must still shade off into the unknown. But we may at least endeavour to trace what we can see of their real outline, to quicken our sense of their positive contents, to deepen our convictions of their absolute and unchanging significance, to enhance the influence which they already exert over our moral natures. It is not well that such topics should be approached with no higher purpose than that of an intellectual enterprise. If we do not mean the cry, "Shew Thou me the way that I should walk in, for I lift up my soul unto Thee," it were better not to enter on the holy ground. Religion indeed must always command the attention of practical men, because it is, at least, one of the most powerful forces, because it shapes the strongest passions, that can govern the conduct of large masses of mankind. It also will ever be interesting to serious thinkers, whether they accept its authority or not; for without controversy it has a word to say upon the highest objects of human thought. But for those who look at it, not only from without but from within, not as a toy of the intellect, but as a necessity of the soul, it must be something more than this. If there be any truth in its teachings at all, if its aspirations be anything more than a waste of heart and effort, lavished through centuries upon what are after all only weird or graceful phantoms of the brain, then nothing that can occupy our thoughts can really compare with it in point of absorbing and momentous import. Beyond everything else, it must have imperious claims upon the time and thought and working power of every human being who has ever felt, in any serious degree, the unspeakable solemnity of life and death. May God endow us with a sense of this interest in that which binds us to Himself, or may He deepen it; and then, in answer to the longings which in every sincere soul it will assuredly foster, may He this Lent be merciful to us, each and all, and bless us, and shew us the light of His countenance, and be merciful unto us![1]

[1] Ps. lxvii. 1.

LECTURE II.

Second Sunday in Lent.

GOD, THE OBJECT OF RELIGION.

Ps. xlii. 2.

My soul is athirst for God, yea even for the living God: when shall I come to appear before the presence of God?

THERE is scarcely, even in the Psalter, a more touching psalm than this. The Psalmist is probably an exile of the early Assyrian period. In the land of his captivity, he is surrounded by all the institutions of an established idolatry, and, as he sadly reflects, he is far removed from the Holy Home of the race of Israel; from the place which the Lord had chosen to put His name there; from the worship and fellowship of the sacred commonwealth. His thought spans the intervening desert, and he dwells with a full and aching heart on all that lies beyond it. He remembers the festival services in Jerusalem in bygone years, when he went with the "multitude keeping holyday," when he, too, had his share in the "voice of joy and praise." As he calls up in memory this cherished part, he pours out his soul in secret grief; and while the cruel heathen around taunt him with the insulting question, Where is thy God? he can only find refuge in tears; his tears, as he tells us, flow by day and by night. When will the long years of exile have an end? When will he come to "appear before the presence of God"? He is like the thirsty stag, panting after the distant water-brooks; his inmost being is "athirst for God, yea even for the living God."

"The living God!" What a strange, yet what a pregnant phrase! Surely, the Author of Life must live; yet here is an expression which hints at the idea of deities who are not alive. It was thus that the Hebrews distinguished the true God Who had revealed Himself to their ancestors from the false gods of the nations around them. "As for all the gods of the heathen, they are but idols; but it is the Lord that made the heavens."[1] The heathen deities were so much carving, sculpture, and colouring; or they were so much human imagination or human speculation; they had no being independent of the toil, whether of the hands or of the brains of men. They had no existence in themselves; they did not live, whether men thought about them or not: as we should say, they had no objective existence. It was true that evil spirits, by lurking beneath the idol forms, or draping themselves in the debasing fancies of the heathen world, might contrive to appropriate the homage which the human heart in its darkness lavished upon its own creations; and thus the Canaanites are said, in their cruel Moloch-worship, to have sacrificed their sons and their

[1] Ps. xcvi. 5.

daughters unto devils.[1] But the broad contrast, latent in the expression "the living God," is the contrast between imagination and fact; between an Existing Being and a collection of fancy personages; between a solemn truth and a stupid and debasing unreality.

We are not here concerned to inquire what elements of truth there may have been in the forms of heathen worship with which the Jews came into contact.[2] Some truth there certainly was in the most degraded of them; since a religion which is pure undiluted falsehood could not continue to exist as a religion, and the false religions which do exist, only exist by virtue of the elements of truth which in varying proportions they severally contain. The lowest fetichism witnesses to the great truth, that man must go out of himself in order to seek for an adequate object of his heart-felt devotion—of his highest enthusiasms. And no instructed Christian would deny that certain forms of heathenism embrace incidentally the recognition of considerable districts of fundamental truth. If, indeed, as S. Paul says, God teaches all men up to a certain point through nature and conscience,[3] it could not be otherwise; and this intermixture of truth, which is thus latent in all heathenism,

[1] Ps. cvi. 37.

[2] On the "Dispensation of Paganism," see Newman's "Arians of the Fourth Century," pp. 87-91; and the quotation from S. Clem. Alex. Strom. vii. 2. "He (the Word) it is who gives to the Greeks their philosophy. . . . His revelations, both the former and the latter, are drawn forth from one fount; those who were before the Law, not suffered to be without Law; those who do not hear the Jewish philosophy, not surrendered to an unbridled course."

[3] Rom. i. 19, 20.

yields the best starting-point for convincing heathens of the errors which they admit, and of the truths which they deny beyond.[1] In this sense, undoubtedly, the science, which has been of late named Comparative Theology, may be made really serviceable to the interests of Christian truth. It is a widely different thing to start with an assumption that all the positive religions in the world, the Jewish and Christian revelations included, are alike conglomerate formations in very varying degrees, partly true and partly false; and that the religion of the future—an etherealized abstraction, to be distilled by science from all the creeds and worships of mankind—will be something beyond, and distinct from all of them. Certainly heathenism is not treated, either in the Old Testament or in the New, with the tenderness which would befit such an anticipation as this. Practically speaking, and as contrasted with the revealed truth, whether Jewish or Christian, heathenism is represented as a lie. To live within its territorial range is to live in the kingdom of darkness;[2] to practise its rites is to be an enemy to God by wicked works;[3] to go after false gods is to have the earnest of great trouble,[4] and to provoke the anger of the real Lord of the Universe. The Assyrian idols did not raise in the exile's mind any question as to the stray elements of truth which might be underlying so much tawdry and impure error. "My soul," he cried, "is athirst for God, yea even

[1] So S. Clem. Alex. speaks of Greek philosophy as ὑποβάθραν οὖσαν τῆς κατὰ Χριστὸν φιλοσοφίας.—Strom. vi., qu. by Newman, ubi sup.

[2] Is. lx. 2; 1 Pet. ii. 9.

[3] Col. i. 21.

[4] Ps. lxxviii. 59, 60; cvi. 36-40.

for the living God: when shall I come to appear before the presence of God?"

The language of this exile is in truth the language of the human heart, under the stress of the purest and deepest desire that man can know. In this life man is an exile; he is parted from his true home and country; he is the victim of an unconquerable restlessness. This restlessness of the mind—this "wasting fever of the heart" of man—this unwillingness to be satisfied with any earthly good—attracted the attention of ancient thinkers. But they did not understand its secret. They would fain have accounted for it by pointing to some fatal warp or flaw in human nature; or they would have silenced it by the tentative guesses of successive philosophies, moving in cycles which ended in proclaiming that nothing beyond the province of sense is trustworthy; or they would have buried it beneath the cares of business, or the cares of empire, or the grosser attractions of sensual pleasure. But again and again the human heart has protested against these endeavours to crush the noblest of its aspirations; and history again and again has echoed with the cry, "My soul is athirst," not for pleasures which may degrade, nor yet for philosophies which may disappoint, but for the Pure, the Absolute, the Everlasting Being. "My soul is athirst for God: when shall I come to appear before the presence of God?"

Was this cry ever heard more distinctly by those who have ears to hear the voices of the spiritual world than in our own generation? The passion, or, as the Psalmist phrases it, the thirst for God—the strong desire of the soul mounting towards Him with all the agonized earnestness of a disappointed and tortured sense—speaks, not merely or chiefly in churches and pulpits, but in magazines, in newspapers, in social gatherings, in political assemblies, with a fervour and decision which would have startled the age of George III. The pulse of this desire is felt outside the Christian camp; it quickens the very enthusiasms of error and paradox; often enough, it mistakes friends for foes and foes for friends; but it is generally sincere, vehement, intolerant of delay and trifling. "My soul is athirst for God, yea even for the living God," is the desire of desires; it really underlies and explains all others that are not purely brutal in this Europe, this England of the nineteenth century. Let us see how it fares—this thirst for God—at the hands of some great speculative systems which more particularly challenge attention in the present day.

I.

High in the world of thought, if we determine its place by the intellectual forces which it can at present muster, while we refuse to adopt any truer and worthier rule of measurement, lies the camp of the Materialists. Materialism is sometimes digested into a system; sometimes it is little more than an intellectual tendency. Occasionally it displays the constructive enthusiasm together with the stiff, and, perhaps, pedantic livery of Positivism: more frequently, it is shy of committing itself to positive theories, while it is consistently earnest in resenting all attempts to base knowledge upon anything besides the verdict of sense. It bids us believe what we can see and smell, and taste and touch; it invites us to make such generalizations as we can out of the report which our senses bring to us. Thus, it assures us, will the mighty universe in which we live reveal itself to us; and we shall learn to perceive in it two, and only two, elements in the last analysis,—a kingdom of matter, that is apparently eternal, unceasingly, infinitely modified by eternal force. How this force and that matter came to be, it knows not: it affirms, as it denies nothing. A philosophy that is positive does not concern itself with the origin of the universe, "if it ever had one," or with what happens to living beings after their death.[1] Of this eternal interfusion of force with matter, man himself is only a ripe and very complex product. There is nothing in him for which his chemistry cannot give an account: his intelligence is exactly proportioned to the mass of his brain: his thought is "but the expression of molecular changes in the physical matter of his life:"[2] his thought is impossible without phosphorus; his consciousness is only a property of matter:[3] his virtue is the result of a current of electri-

[1] Paroles de Philosophie Positive, p. 31, qu. by Bp. Dupanloup.
[2] Fortn. Rev., 1869.
[3] Büchner, Kraft und Stoft, § 122. Ohne Phosphor kein Gedanke, ... auch das Bewusstsein ist nichts als eine Eigenschaft des Stoffes.

city; his virtue and his vice are strictly due to his natural organization, they are "products in the same sense as are sugar and vitriol." All that he can do, either with himself or with the world around him, is to search out and to register the several qualities of matter, and to number and measure the ever-shifting forms of the force which governs it. There may be something beyond matter and force —who knows? But science, which deals only with positive realities, cannot concern herself with, as she does not need, "such an hypothesis" as God. Can God be verified by the senses? Is He not a phantom that belongs properly to the childhood of humanity? Is He not an anachronism in a scientific age?[1] What is He, then, whom men commonly name God? God, says Feuerbach, whose Pantheism is really Materialism, is only "the nature of man regarded as absolute truth;" "that which is given to man's God, is in truth given to man himself;" "what a man declares concerning God, he in truth declares concerning himself;" "the Divine activity is not distinct from the human;" "in God man has only his own activity as an object;" "the mystery of the inexhaustible fulness of the Divine predicates is nothing else than the mystery of human nature considered as an infinitely varied, infinitely modifiable, but consequently phenomenal being."[2] In other words, God does not exist apart from the mind and imagination of man; He is only its creation, and has no

[1] See Conservation, Révolution, Positivisme, p. 70, qu. by Dupanloup, l'Athéisme, p. 70.

[2] Feuerbach, Geist des Christenthums, § 2.

rightful place in the region of serious and scientific thought.

This is not, I trust, a misrepresentation of the language of contemporary Materialism: and whatever else may be said of it, this at least is certain, that it does nothing whatever towards satisfying that great desire or "thirst" for communion with a Higher Being, of which, in his best and highest moods, man is so profoundly conscious. It denies, if not that any such being really exists, at least that we can know Him to be really existing. They who have no satisfaction to offer to a need naturally condemn the demand for one: they who have no answer to give, would rather not be questioned. And yet the religious side of man's nature is a fact of which a philosophy of experience should surely take account. Upon what is man's religious instinct to spend itself in the Materialistic universe? Upon that phantom-god who, as we are told, is only a pale reflection of human vanity? But the soul asks for reality, and cannot occupy itself with a confessed shadow. Upon that eternal flux of self-existent matter? upon that ceaseless activity of self-existing force? But is there anything in mere force or matter, or in both combined, I will not say to satisfy a passion which is purest and strongest in saintly men, but even to have any contact with or relation towards it whatever? How can that which is purely physical touch the sense which appreciates a moral world? It is a merit of Auguste Comte to have recognized the necessity of some answer; and he tells us that it is our privilege and our business to love, reverence, and worship " a Being, immense and eternal—Humanity."[1] Not, mark you, a sinless and Divine representative of the race, such as we Christians adore in the Incarnate Jesus, seated as He is at the right hand of the Father. Not even an idealized abstraction, which, in the pure realms of thought, might conceivably be separated from the weaknesses and degradations of the sum-total of human flesh and blood. But this very collective human family itself, in all ages and of all conditions, viewed as one organism; this human family, not merely illuminated by its struggles, its sufferings, its victories, but also weighted with its crimes, its brutalities, its deep and hideous degradations. It might be thought that " we men know man too well to care to worship him." Yet, seriously, this is the god who is to supersede the Most Holy Trinity, when Positivism has won its way to empire in European thought. Will he, think you, satisfy the mighty thirst of the human soul? What does this thirst mean but man's endeavour to escape from himself, to rise to an ideal, or rather to a reality above himself, to lose himself in a Being who is greater, wiser, better than himself? Yet here he is bidden, in the name, if without the sanction of the most recent science, to seek the object of his trust and worship within himself, since nothing higher than himself is really cognizable by his understanding. It is clear that teachers who do not believe in a living God must leave one side, and that the highest, of human

[1] Cat. Pos. Int.

nature altogether uncared for; since in truth they have nothing to say to it. And history does not smile upon materialistic attempts to bribe the religious yearnings of the soul of man. Atheism could indeed, on one fatal day, throne naked vice as the goddess Reason upon the high altar of a Christian basilica, while an apostate archbishop lent his presence to the hideous ceremony; but it was one thing to obey the interested or sentimental fanaticism of the Jacobin Clubs, and quite another permanently to control the heart and convictions even of the Voltairianized multitudes of Paris.[1] The realities of religion might have been hated; but this godless parody of worship could only provoke a languid contempt.

II.

Against Materialism, in all its forms, the common sense of man, not to speak of his religious instinct, will ever protest. The idea or presentiment of God, everywhere rooted in the mind of man, is a fact sufficiently important to be treated as something better than a superstition by those who put forward any serious doctrine about human

[1] Pressensé, L'Eglise et la Révolution Française, p. 280. "Il ne resta de ce jour que le souvenir d'une stupide parodie qui vengeait à elle seule la religion sainte que l'on avait voulu fouler aux pieds. C'est en vain que pour ranimer la ferveur on remplaça à Paris et dans les départements les actrices par les prostituées. L'ennui et le dégoût frappèrent le nouveau culte dès ses débuts.

E

nature. A mental fact is as worthy of attention as any fact which can be appraised in a chemical laboratory or on the roof of an observatory. Cicero's statement[1] that there is no nation so barbarous and wild as not to have believed in some divinity, is still, notwithstanding certain apparent exceptions, true. A nation of pure Atheists is yet to be discovered.[2] Unworthy and degraded as are many of the beliefs on the subject of a Higher Power that are to be found in the heathen world, some groping after the Great Unseen, some tentative intuition, some shadowy belief there is to be found always and everywhere. Man thinks of a Higher Power as naturally as he thinks of the world

[1] Cic. de Legibus, i. 8. Itaque ex tot generibus nullum est animal præter hominem quod habeat notitiam aliquam dei: ipsisque in hominibus nulla gens est neque tam immansueta neque tam fera, quæ non, etiam si ignorat qualem habere deum deceat, tamen habendum sciat. Tuscul. Disput., i. 13. Ut porro firmissimum hoc afferri videtur, cur deos esse credamus, quod nulla gens tam fera, nemo omnium tam sit immanis, cujus mentem non imbuerit deorum opinio:—multi de diis prava sentiunt (id enim vitioso more effici solet); omnes tamen esse vim et naturam divinam arbitrantur: nec vero id collocutio hominum aut consensus effecit; non institutis opinio est confirmata, non legibus. Omni autem in re consentio omnium gentium lex naturæ putanda est.

[2] Cf. Diderot, Philosophie des Canadiens. Œuvres, I. p. 433. Max Müller, "Chips from a German Workshop." "There is perhaps no race of men so low and degraded as the Papuas. It has frequently been asserted that they have no religion at all, and yet these same Papuas, if they want to know whether what they are going to undertake is right or wrong, squat before their karwar, clasp the hands over the forehead, and bow repeatedly, at the same time stating their intentions. If they are seized with any nervous feeling during this time, it is considered as a bad sign, and the project is abandoned for a time; if otherwise, the idol is supposed to approve. Here we have but to translate what they in their helpless language call 'nervous feeling' by our word 'conscience,' and we shall not only understand what they really mean, but confess, perhaps, that it would be well for us if, in our own hearts, the karwar occupied the same prominent place which it occupies in the cottage of every Papua."

around him, or of himself. Nay, he thinks of Truth; and truth is no mere abstraction; it is a Real Being; it is God.[1] He thinks of the Infinite, says Fenelon, as he thinks of the circle, of the line, of the distinction between whole and part.[2] The spontaneous activity of his consciousness brings with it, contains in itself, the thought of One who is greater, if not also stronger, wiser, better than all else; and that man should thus think of Him, is of itself a presumption that He really exists.[3] This instinctive perception and affirmation of God is indeed not merely an act of the intellect; it is also, as will be insisted on presently, perhaps it is chiefly, an act of the moral sense, an act of the conscience. It is that upward attraction of the

[1] Plat. Repub. vii. 517.

[2] De l'existence de Dieu, 1ere partie, p. 60. L'idée de l'infini est en moi comme celle des nombres, des lignes, des cercles, d'un tout et d'une partie. Changer nos idées ce serait anéantir la raison même.

[3] The *ontological* "argument" for the existence of God is stated in varying degrees of completeness by S. Augustine, Boethius, S. Anselm, and Descartes. To cite the two last, S. Ans. Proslog. 2, convincitur etiam insipiens (Ps. xiv. 1) esse vel in intellectu aliquid quo nihil majus cogitari potest. Et certè id quo majus cogitari nequit non potest esse in intellectu solo. Si enim vel in solo intellectu est, potest cogitari esse et in re quod majus est. Si ergo id quo majus cogitari non potest est in intellectu; id ipsum, quo majus cogitari non potest est quo majus cogitari potest: sed certè hoc esse non potest. Existit ergo procul dubio aliquid quo majus cogitari non valet, et in intellectu et in re. Descartes observes (Medit. de Prim. Philos. 3, 4, sub fin.) "notiones nostras esse aut adventitias, aut factitias, aut innatas. Ideam de Deo non esse adventitiam, Deum enim non experientiâ duce reperiri; neque factitiam, nam non arbitrio a nobis effictam esse; ergo esse innatam, sive a Deo ipso nobis suppeditatam." This is undoubtedly the weakest of the arguments for God's existence; but its real value should not be mistaken on account of the facility with which it lends itself to the Hegelian doctrine that "God is only God in so far as He has knowledge of Himself; but His self-knowledge is 'sein selbst bewusstseyn in Menschen und das Wissen des Menschen von Gott'" (Encycl. p. 576, qu. by Grimm).

soul upon which Plato dilates;[1] it is the universal hypothesis which Aristotle registers;[2] it is the world-wide prejudice of Epicurus; it is the "anticipation" naturally imbedded in the human mind, of Cicero.[3] It precedes demonstration; it is out of the reach of criticism; it resists hostile argument. It is, speaking philosophically, a fact in psychological science, and a fact so fruitful and stimulating, that to it must be traced all in human life and effort that looks really upward,—man's love of truth, his clinging to a coming life, his aspirations to rise above the level of animal existence. It is, speaking religiously, in its way, a revelation; it is a revelation of God within, as S. Paul says, answering to the revelation of God from without; it sets man's thought in motion as he gazes upon the natural world, and bids him not to rest until he has wrung from it a disclosure of the highest truth which it has to teach him.

And thus, with this preparatory idea or intuition of a Divinity, the human mind approaches what are called the

[1] Cf. the whole passage in Plato, de Legibus, ix. x. 899, c. d. e., qu. by Staudenmaier, Dogm. II. 22.

[2] Arist. de Cœlo, 1-3. *πάντες γὰρ ἄνθρωποι περὶ θεῶν ἔχουσιν ὑπόληψιν, καὶ πάντες τὸν ἀνωτάτω τῷ θείῳ τόπον ἀποδιδόασι.* Referred to by Staudenmaier, ubi. sup.

[3] Cic. de Nat. Deorum, i. 16. Solus enim vidit [Epicurus] primum esse deos, quod in omnium animis eorum notionem impressisset ipsa natura. Quæ est enim gens, aut quod genus hominum, quod non habeat sine doctrinâ anticipationem quandam decorum? quam appellat *πρόληψιν* Epicurus, id est anteceptam animo rei quandam informationem, sine quâ nec intelligi quidquam, nec quæri, nec disputari potest. Cujus rationis vim atque utilitatem ex illo cœlesti Epicuri de regulâ et judicio volumine accepimus.

proofs of God's existence. Looking out upon the universe around it, the mind seeks for its productive cause.[1] Whatever efforts may have been made by recent writers to reduce causation to mere antecedence, the law of causation is at once a primary law of human thought and of the world without us.[2] What cause, what force, preceded and brought into existence this universe? All the causes with which we come in contact here, are, as we term them, second causes; but they point to a cause beyond themselves, to a cause of causes, to a supreme all-producing Cause, Itself uncaused, unoriginate. The heavenly bodies move on unceasingly in their orbits, obedient to the laws of gravitation, but no law of gravitation could have assigned them their place in space.[3] The whole universe bids us look beyond itself for the adequate explanation of its existence. "So far is it from being true," says Lord Bacon, "that the

[1] The *cosmological* proof of God's existence is stated with great beauty and variety of illustration by Fenelon, Traité de l'existence et des Attributs de Dieu, c. 1, 2. To the original form of the argument which, looking upon the world as an effect, seeks for its cause, Leibnitz adds a second, based upon the *contingent* nature of the world and its several parts, which obliges us to seek in the πρῶτον κινοῦν, or First Cause, the Unchanging and intrinsically Necessary Being. This Necessary Being is not, as Strauss says, the "ewiges Grundwesen der Welt," or the permanent material of the universe, as distinct from its ever-changing forms; because the necessity of seeking a first cause obliges us to go beyond the universe, which, as a whole, is an effect. On the other hand, the cosmological argument does not of itself lead us to a moral God, such as would satisfy the instincts of piety—the "thirst" of the soul.

[2] Cf. M'Cosh, "Method of the Divine Government," Appendices III. and IV.

[3] Newton, Philos. Nat. Princip. L. III. schol. gen. Perseverabunt quidem in orbibus suis per leges gravitatis, sed regularem orbium situm primitus acquirire per has leges minimè potuerunt.

explanation of phenomena by natural causes leads us away from God and His Providence, that those philosophers who have passed their lives in discovering such causes can find nothing that affords a final explanation without having recourse to God and His Providence."[1] The father of the inductive philosophy does but speak the common sense of religion; but will it be maintained, except by writers who are prepared to deny the existence of causation, that he does not also utter the common sense of scientific thought?

Does the universe tell us anything as to the nature of its First Cause? Surely we may at least presume that the Author of the natural world must be higher and greater than anything in the natural world.[2] Water will not rise above its source; and it is inconceivable that, if there be an Author of nature at all, His Self-existent Life must not be higher and nobler than any life which He has bestowed. Who does not see the force of the Psalmist's argument, "He that made the ear, shall He not hear? and He that gave the eye, shall He not see?"[3] Above the life of the

[1] De Augm. Scient., iii. 4. Adeo ut tantum absit ut causæ physicæ hominem à Deo et Providentiâ abducant, ut contra potiùs philosophi illi qui in iisdem eruendis occupati fuerunt, nullum exitum rei reperiant, nisi postremò ad Deum et providentiam confugiant.

[2] That the one true God may be known from His works in Nature is taught, as against Gentile idolatry, in Isaiah xliv.; xlv. 18, *sqq.*; Acts xiv. 15-17; xvii. 22, *sqq.*; Rom. i. 19-20. That the natural world witnesses to the beauty of His Being and Attributes is implied in Psalms viii. 2-4; xix. 1, *sqq.*; civ., passim, &c. Holy Scripture, of course, does not demonstrate the existence of Him Whose true Nature it unveils; but it points to the natural world as involving for all reasoning beings the privilege and the responsibility of some knowledge of its Author's existence, and of His character.

[3] Ps. xciv. 9.

tree, there is that of the animal; above that of the animal, there is the life of man. Man, with all his ingenuity and will, cannot produce a leaf or a shell-fish: and is it to be supposed that the author of man's life is less endowed with thought and volition than man? We may paraphrase the Psalmist: He That made the human intellect, shall He not think? And how came it to exist, if He did not make it?[1] There are chasms in the natural world which no theories substituting a fated self-development for the free action of God will really bridge over. There is the chasm between the inorganic and the organic; the chasm between the lifeless and that which lives; the chasm between animal instinct and the reflective consciousness. At each of these levels of creation we seem to feel more sensibly than elsewhere the fresh intervention of a creating Intelligence; and our conviction of His activity is strengthened when we observe the interdependence and harmony of the universe as a whole, in which each part is necessary, in which nothing is really out of place, and between the several elements of which new relations are continually coming to light, as if to justify His foresight and to enhance our estimate of His inexhaustible resources.[2] "Those

[1] Bossuet, Œuv. i. 79. Si nous étions tous seuls intelligents dans le monde, nous seuls nous vaudrions mieux avec notre intelligence imparfaite, que toute la reste, qui serait tout-a-fait brute et stupide, et on ne pourrait comprehendre d'ou viendrait dans ce tout qui n'entend pas cette partie qui entend, l'intelligence ne pouvant nâitre d'une chose brute et insensée.

[2] The *teleological* argument for the existence of God, which sees a purpose in the forces and laws of the natural world, and in the events of human history, has been chiefly discredited in modern times by the popular supposition that modern attacks upon the doctrine of final causes have been really

persons," says Montesquieu, "who maintain that a blind fate has produced all the effects we see in the world, maintain that which is a great absurdity; for what absurdity can be greater than a blind fate producing intelligent beings?"[1] How do you know, a Bedouin was asked, that there is a God? "In the same way," he replied, "that I know, on looking at the sand, when a man or a beast has crossed the desert—by His footprints in the world around me."

III.

Thus does the common sense or reason of man lead him up to recognizing One Supreme Intelligence as at least the original cause of all that he is and sees around him. But then the question arises, what is the relation that actually subsists between this Highest Intelligence and the universe? To this question there are two leading answers.

successful. For a partial and popular consideration of some recent objections to Final Causes, urged by Mr. Herbert Spencer, Mr. Lewes, and others, cf. M'Cosh, Christianity and Positivism, pp. 78–88. Even if a doctrine of evolution should in time be accepted as scientifically, and so as theologically certain, such a doctrine would not be inconsistent either with that belief in the original act of creation which is essential to Theism, or with "the recognition of plan and purpose in the number and variety of animated beings." "Evolution," from a Theistic point of view, is merely our way of describing what we can observe of God's continuous action upon the physical world; and because the phrase seems tacitly or poetically to invest the universe with a power of self-unfolding, it does not follow that the question of an Intelligent Creator and Ruler is thereby decided in the negative by those who employ it.

[1] Esprit des Lois. Cf. Ps. xiv. 1.

The Deist so far agrees with the Christian, as to admit that God is related to the world as its Creator; and that He must have made it out of nothing by the fiat of His Will. But with this admission—momentous as it is—the old Deism practically closes its account of God's free personal action upon His work. Since the creation, God's action is represented as being practically superseded by a system of unchangeable routine; and this routine is conceived to be so strictly invariable, as to bind the liberty of the presumed Agent. The Deistic theory of the universe might remind us of the relations which, at least until some very recent events, were understood to exist between the Government of Egypt and the Sublime Porte. There was occasionally a formal recognition of the sovereign power on the part of the nominal dependency, but Egypt was governed by a practically independent Viceroy; the Suzerain's name was mentioned rarely, or only in a formal way; his active influence would have been at once resented, the real power being lodged elsewhere. According to the old Deism, God created the world; but He cannot be supposed ever to interfere with the ordinary laws of its government. He cannot work miracles; He is, in no tangible sense, a Providence. He is well out of the way of active human interests: it is not to be supposed that He can hear the prayer of a worm writhing on one of His planets; that the happiness or misfortunes of a larger sort of animalculæ can give Him any real concern. So He is throned by the Deistic writer in magnificent inactivity at a very remote corner of the universe, while a new power has practically taken His place.

In the last century, at the first great outburst of Deistic thought, Nature practically superseded God. Men talked and wrote persistently about the laws of Nature, the moods of Nature, the religion of Nature: Nature was so vividly and constantly personified in conversation and in literature, that the European world might be supposed to have lighted upon a new goddess, charged, in a very special sense, with the interests of humanity. We live in a more positive and realistic age; and where our fathers talked of Nature, modern Deism names "laws." What is lost in picturesqueness is gained in truth. There is no such person as Nature; but there are observable modes of the Divine activity, which may never vary within the experience of a race. Order is, as Christians know, a characteristic of all God's works; but He, the Almighty, is so little enslaved by the rules which He freely observes, that moment by moment He wills the very order that seems to bind His liberty. Deism, however, really means by "laws"—forces which have become somehow independent of God; fatal forces, which defy His power to innovate upon their resistless play. But what can this impotent Deistic God, from whose control his universe has so escaped as to constitute itself a self-governing machine,—say or do to meet the aspirations, or relieve the despondencies of the human soul? If we cannot love and trust volcanic forces, or vital forces, the laws of growth or the laws of decomposition;

can we love and trust a being who has left this universe to itself; who surveys it, if he does survey it, in the cynicism of an unbroken silence from a very distant throne; to whom its vast oceans of hope and fear, and struggle and disappointment, and triumph and failure—all the mysteries of its moral life, are of no more concern than they are to the rocks and seas around us? No, the god of Deism does not quench the religious thirst of the soul. The soul of man seeks the Living God, not a deity who is as remote from human interests as was the Jupiter of expiring Paganism.

The French Revolution was fertile in religious or irreligious experiments; and as it endeavoured to satisfy the human soul with Atheism, so it made yet more strenuous effort to satisfy it with Deism.[1] Robespierre had publicly

[1] So Alison. Compare Pressensé, l'Eglise et la Révolution, p. 294. La fête eut lieu le 20 prairial. Rien n'avait été épargné pour la rendre grandiose et cependant elle n'évita pas les puérilités ridicules. Robespierre, président de la Convention, en bel habit bleu, avec un bouquet de fruits et d'épis dans les mains, prit place avec tous ses collègues sur l'amphithéâtre élevé au milieu des Tuileries. Après un pompeux discours, il en descendit pour incendier la statue de l'Athéisme, promptement remplacée par celle de la Sagesse qui parut malheureusement très enfumée. Des Tuileries la Convention se rendit au Champ de Mars, entourée et comme enlacée d'un ruban tricolore, que portaient des enfants ornés de violettes, des adolescents ceints de myrtes, des hommes d'âge mûr couronnés de feuilles de chênes et des vieillards parés de pampre et d'olivier. Un char bucolique chargé d'instruments aratoires suivait la Convention, traîné par les inévitables bœufs à cornes dorées et suivi par les non moins inévitables jeunes filles en blanc. Au Champ de Mars la Convention se plaça sur une montagne artificielle, monument flatteur pour les députés de la majorité. Le président pérora, les jeunes filles chantèrent, les vieillards donnèrent leur bénédiction, les canons tonnèrent et tout se termina par le cri de *vive la République*. Ces pompes d'opéra comique, ces symboles ridicules et ces rites glacés apprenaient à la France qu'il est plus facile de décréter un changement de religion que de l'opérer. Jamais le déisme ne fondera un culte et tout ce qu'il essayera dans ce genre tombera

declared that Chaumette deserved death for the abominations which accompanied the Feast of Reason in Notre Dame, on November 7, 1793; and he took a leading part in the Feast of the Supreme Being, which was celebrated in the gardens of the Tuileries and in the Champ de Mars, on June 9, 1794. The Convention decreed that he should discharge the duties of Supreme Pontiff on the occasion. The Deism of Robespierre was sufficiently vivid to admit of his believing that God does rule the affairs of men; he maintained with particular earnestness that God hates kings and priests. The undeniable eloquence of the president of the Convention, the art and industry of the painter David, the music, the costumes, the political enthusiasm at fever height, did all that could be done for the success of the festival. But you cannot lash a multitude into devotion to a remote and hypothetical abstraction by any elaborate display of ceremonial; and the real deity of the occasion was Robespierre. As he marched along, overshadowed with his plumes, and adorned with his tricolor scarf, while the air resounded with cries of "Vive Robespierre," his countenance, says the historian, was radiant with joy. "See how they applaud him," said his colleagues. "He would become a god: he is no longer the High Priest of the Supreme Being." History does not ascribe to this attempt any special efficacy in reviving among the French

sous la risée publique. La fête fut trouvée bien longue, surtout pour ceux qu'irritait le rôle prépondérant de Robespierre. On raconte qu'un représentant moins patient que ses collègues lui dit en termes d'une trivialité énergique: "Tu commences à nous ennuyer avec ton Etre Suprême."

people a sense of their duties towards their forgotten Maker. The most tangible result of the day was the decree proposed by Couthon, for increasing the powers of the Revolutionary Tribunal.

To the question, What is the relation between the universe and the Supreme Intelligence? another and a very different answer has been given. If Deism practically banishes God from the world, Pantheism, at least, sees what it calls God everywhere, and in everything.[1] The Pantheistic god is the common principle which not only is held to constitute the unity of, but which is, the universe. According to Benedict Spinoza,[2] God is the one eternal substance, which makes its appearance in the twofold realm of thought and of matter. Out of it all individual forms of existence are constantly emerging, and like waves upon the ocean, they are as constantly sinking back into, and being absorbed by it, as the common stream of universal life. God alone is, says Fichte, and apart from Him is nothing,[3]—a great truth in one sense, and a great falsehood in another. Hegel teaches that the Absolute is the universal reason; which, after having buried and lost itself in nature, recovers itself in man, in the shape of self-conscious thought. Man's thought of God, therefore, is the true God, the only existing God. God exists only in human thought;

[1] Wegscheider, Inst. p. 240. Pantheismus—ea sententia quâ naturam divinam mundo supponant et Deum ac mundum unum idemque esse statuunt.

[2] Cf. Tractat. de Deo. c. 2. Suppl. ad. opp. Amst. 1862. For his Theory of Substance, cf. Ethic, p. 1, Def. 5.

[3] Fichte, Von Sel. Leben, § 143.

human thought is the reason of nature arriving at self-consciousness. Man thinks of God, and, in man's thinking, God exists; He has no independent or personal existence.[1]

The great attraction and strength of Pantheism lies in the satisfaction which it professes to offer to one very deep and legitimate aspiration; it endeavours to assure man of his real union with the source of his own and of the universal life. It is this profound idea, this most fascinating allurement, that can alone explain the empire, which, in various ages and under various forms, Pantheism has wielded in human history. It inspires Eleatic and Indian philosophies; it is the animating principle of such worship of the generative and life-sustaining powers in nature, as was, for instance, that of the Phœnician Baalim. Since Lessing, Spinoza has almost reigned in certain districts of cultivated Europe, and Germany is by no means the only home of the thought of Schelling and of Hegel. In its later forms Pantheism is, speaking historically, a reaction from and a protest against the older Rationalistic Deism. It often represents a noble plea that God shall not be banished by modern thought from all real contact with humanity: nay, it would fain essay to do in its way what the Divine Incarnation has actually done; it would make men partakers of the Divine Nature. And this, its religious aim, is beyond question a main secret of its power.

[1] Hegel's fundamental error consists in his identification of the "abstract thought" of man with the "Absolute Thought." Fichte (Zeitschrift für Philosophie, Bd. 17, § 292) says that this is "nicht nür höchst willkurlich und grundlos, sondern eine contradictio in adjecto." Qu. by Hettinger; cf. Hegel, Phil. der Rel. §§ 207, 261, 263; Encycl. § 56.

Yet does the Pantheistic deity afford any real satisfaction to the needs of the soul of man? Can he be the object of any serious religious effort whatever? What is there in him to which the life of religion can possibly attach itself? He is not a person: for Pantheism necessarily denies the existence of personality. He is not a cause: for Pantheism cannot tolerate any doctrine of causation. He is not even, as the Absolute Substance, in anywise distinct from phenomena; for, while it is loyal to its central position, Pantheism cannot afford to admit the correctness of such a distinction. What is he then? He is only a fine name for the universe. He has no existence apart from it: he is the universal life, of which you and I are transient manifestations or forms. You may indeed encounter him draped and veiled in a phraseology so reverent and tender, that it might seem to have been borrowed from the inmost shrines of Christian mysticism; but when you force yourself to look at the hard reality beneath, you find that it is practically identical with that presented by Materialism.[1] If God be in reality only the spirit or life of the universe, how can He provoke the yearnings of the soul, or how satisfy its aspirations? How can He be the object, whether of religious homage, or of religious trust? How can we yield love, obedience, worship to a mere torrent of existence that flows onwards inexorably beneath our feet; we, the ripples, who do but rise upon its surface to sink away

[1] Strauss, Gl. 1, § 517. Seine Existenz als wesen ist unser denken von ihm; aber seine reale Existenz ist die Natur, zu welcher das einzelne Denkende als Moment gehört.

after our little moment of undulation? Or how can a sensible and modest man love, trust, worship, his own self-consciousness, under the idea that in each reflecting mind God has become conscious of Himself? Nay, if religion has anything to do with reverence for goodness and with abhorrence of moral evil, if it is not a sentiment that has been rendered by modern speculation wholly independent of moral truth, how can we worship either an inner self into which, as we must each of us know, evil penetrates so constantly and so pervadingly; or an universal life of which in its highest, that is its human, manifestation, evil is, as a matter of fact, more frequently an accompaniment than good? How, I say, can such an absolute principle be the object of religion, if its activity be manifested not less truly in murder and lust than in heroism and unselfishness; if the darkest forms of evil stand to it in a relation just as necessary as do the highest forms of good; if by it, in a word, all moral distinctions whatever are really annihilated?

Between Pantheism and an earnest hatred of moral evil there is accordingly a necessary opposition, and this reason alone establishes a permanent divorce between it and any true effort at communion with the All-Pure, such as all that is best in us enjoins. But further, that which in a Christian, as in any earnest Theist, makes Pantheism impossible, is the first article of his creed: "I believe in God the Father Almighty, *Maker* of heaven and earth." As the act of creation was not witnessed, so it cannot be demonstrated. "By faith we understand that the worlds were made by the word of God."[1] Creation interposes an immeasurable chasm between the Creator and the creature; between that Pure and Awful Life Which is indebted to none else either for existence or support, and this life of dependence, weakness, corruption. And belief in creation is a necessary outwork of any true theism whatever: deny

[1] Heb. xi. 3. That God created the universe is the first truth which Scripture teaches us about Him, Gen. i. 1. Cf. Job xxxviii. 4-7; Ps. xxxiii. 6-9, thus revealing His majestic beauty; Ps. xix. 1-7; xcvii. 1-6; cxix. 64. The Jews knew that this creation involved not merely the bringing order and life, *ἐξ ἀμόρφου ὕλης*, Wisd. xi. 17, but also originally the calling this formless material itself into being, *ἐξ οὐκ ὄντων*, 2 Mac. vii. 28. In the New Testament, creation is generally referred to as furnishing arguments for moral truths or duties; as by our Lord, Matt. xix. 4-6, for its witness to the indissolubility of the marriage tie; and by S. Paul, as yielding proof of God's real relation to the world, Acts xvii. 24; or of His interest in the whole human family, and of our duty of seeking Him, *ib.* 26; for the refutation of a false dualistic asceticism, 1 Tim. iv. 3; cf. Eph. iv. 6. That He has created all things and for Himself is His title to praise and adoration, Rev. iv. 11. Although the New Testament does not in express terms speak of creation out of nothing, it implies this truth. S. Paul's arguments in Acts xvii. 24, and 1 Tim. iv. 3, would lose their force, if it were true that God was not the maker of matter as well as the artist who gave it form, while the doxology of Rev. iv. 11 could not be truthfully addressed to a Being who had not created matter, or who had formed anything out of pre-existent material which he did not create. The *ἄμορφος ὕλη* of S. Justin Martyr (Apol. i. 10), and even the *ὕλη ἄχρονος* of Clement (Phot. Bibl. cod. 109) is not necessarily eternal; the creation of matter out of nothing, and of the world out of matter, were distinct events, separated by intervals that distance all human thought. Tertullian pointed out that Hermogenes, in teaching the eternity of matter, was really a Ditheist (Adv. Herm. c. 4.) The general teaching of the ancient church is expressed by S. Augustine (De fid. et symb. c. 2): Credimus omnia Deum fecisse de nihilo, quia, etiamsi de aliquâ materiâ factus est mundus, eadem ipsa materia de nihilo facta est, ut ordinatissimo Dei munere primo capacitas formarum fieret, ac deinde formarentur quæcunque formata sunt. Hoc autem diximus, ne quis existimet contrarias sibi esse Scripturarum sententias: quoniam et omnia Deum fecisse de nihilo scriptum est, et mundum esse factum de informi materiâ.

F

creation and you deny God. If God in His unfettered freedom did not summon into existence all that is, if the universe escaped from Him against His will, He is not alone the Omnipotent: if anything that we term matter or spirit has from the beginning co-existed side by side with Him, He is not alone the Eternal.[1] The difficulty is not met by phrases about the eternal Idea passing into reality; since it will be asked how such a passage could have been effected, or rather, why it should have taken place at all? A creative Will having no limits to its power, is at least intelligible, but the mind refuses to dwell seriously on such a process as a transmutation of thought into matter. In its attempt to explain itself, Pantheism practically sinks back into Materialism; it has no expedients equal to the task of saving its god from burial beneath the materialistic chaos of matter and force.

Will it be said that to believe in a Creator-God is to close the eye to the presence of God in creation? But who that believes in the Omnipresent can limit His presence? Is not the original act of creation a warrant for the Creator's continued presence with and action upon His work?[2] The Apostle who taught the Athenians that God made the world and all things therein, taught them also, and in the same great sermon, that "He is not far from every

[1] Cf. S. Aug. Conf. xii. 7. Fecisti cœlum et terram non de Te, nam esset æquale Unigenito Tuo, et aliud præter Te non erat, unde faceres, ideo de nihilo fecisti cœlum et terram. S. Iren. Hær. ii. 10, 4. Homines quidem de nihilo non possunt aliquid facere, sed de materiâ subjacenti: Deus autem materiam fabricationis suæ, cum ante non esset, ipse adinvenit.

[2] S. John v. 17.

one of us, for in Him we live and move and have our being."[1] To assert God's presence in His works is one thing; to identify Him with them is another. His omnipresence is a necessary attribute of His Deity; while if He could be identified with nature He would cease to be. If the mystery of life, which attests God's presence in the natural world, was ever felt in all its awe and its beauty by any human soul, it was felt by the great Augustine. Witness the often quoted passage of the Confessions in which he tells us why nature was in his eyes so beautiful, by telling us how nature had led him up to God. "I asked the earth, and it said: 'I am not He;' and all that is upon it made the same confession. I asked the sea and the depths, and the creeping things that have life, and they answered: 'We are not thy God; look thou above us.' I asked the breezes and the gales; and the whole air, with its inhabitants, said to me: 'Anaximenes is in error, I am not God.' I asked the heaven, the sun, the moon, the stars: 'We too,' said they, 'are not the God Whom thou seekest.' And I said to all the creatures that surround the doors of my fleshly senses, 'Ye have said to me of my God that ye are not He; tell me somewhat of Him.' And with a great voice, they exclaimed 'He made us.'"[2]

[1] Acts xvii. 27, 28.

[2] S. Aug. Conf. x. 6. Interrogavi terram et dixit: non sum; et quæcumque in eâdem sunt idem confessa sunt. Interrogavi mare et abyssos et reptilia animarum vivarum, et responderunt: Non sumus Deus tuus, quære super nos. Interrogavi auras flabiles, et inquit universus aër cum incolis suis: Fallitur Anaximenes, non sum Deus. Interrogavi cœlum, solem, lunam, stellas: Neque nos sumus Deus quem quæris, inquiunt. Et dixi

IV.

So long as the human mind only conceives of God as a Supreme Intelligence, it will oscillate hesitatingly between these two errors; between a sterile Deism which banishes God from the world, and a reactionary Pantheism which buries Him in it. It is when we gain a height beyond, and observe the third great form of argument with which man clothes and fortifies his presentiment of God, that we are saved from this liability. Here a view of God's Nature opens out upon us, which is at once conservative of His moral Purity and distinctness from created life, and which also does justice to the intimacy of His contact with the world and with humanity.

The philosopher of Konigsberg, who in his Critique of Pure Reason has made the most of some well-known objections against those arguments for God's existence, which are drawn from the existence and structure of the universe,[2] insists with great force upon the strength of the inference by which the human conscience ascends to the recognition of God. If Kant is a sceptic in the domain of speculative thought, his doubts vanish altogether when, entering that of the practical reason, as he terms it, he listens to the commands of moral truth.[1] This practical reason is wholly independent of any discovery or decision external to itself:

omnibus iis quæ circumstant fores carnis meæ: Dixistis mihi de Deo meo quod vos non estis, dicite mihi de illo aliquid. Et exclamaverunt voce magnâ: Ipse fecit nos.

[1] Luthardt, Apologet. Vortr. L. iii. Scholten, Phil. in Rel., p. 100.

[2] Kritik d. reinen Vernunft, Abt. ii. B. 2, kap. 3, §§ 4, 5, 6.

it apprehends the good as such without waiting for the judgment of experience. Its commands are issued without limit or reserve; they have an objective certainty; they "judge all things, while they themselves are judged of no man." They lead us to recognize as necessary truths, first, the freedom of man's will; next, a future life; thirdly, the existence of God. The voice of the practical reason, "Thou oughtest," implies "Thou canst"; the categorical imperative is meaningless in the absence of moral freedom. Man is free, and his conscience perpetually affirms that he must do good at all costs, even although doing good should not make him happy. It affirms no less clearly that if he is really virtuous he should be happy. Yet, in the experience of life, the good man who does good is often unhappy, while vice is not unfrequently salaried and crowned with rewards that are denied to virtue. The sight of this contradiction forces the conscience to infer a life to come, and a Moral Being Who, in His justice, will re-establish those relations between happiness and virtue which it persistently recognizes as necessary. Thus the practical reason reaches God, not by a demonstration of His existence, but as a postulate of its own activity. Speculation may mislead, but duty is a certainty; and duty is no arbitrary creation either of our reason, or of our self-interest; it is not an abstraction which rests on nothing beyond itself; it is out of the reach of merely speculative criticism, yet it leads us to the Master of the moral world. Those clear, precise, categorical orders which are imposed in varying degrees of urgency upon all human wills, point to a really living Ruler of men, in Whom man cannot disbelieve without doing violence to himself. Certainly Kant would have had little patience with the theory that conscience itself is only a collection of prejudices received from childhood, and incorporated with the moral life; that it is simply the result of early training, and has no real basis in the soul. For this theory confuses the furniture of the conscience with the conscience itself; the acquisitions of a faculty with its existence. It might be contended with equal justice that the human mind does not exist because it is developed by exercise, and enlarged by information.[1] Certainly conscience may be enlightened or it may be misinformed by education. But the original faculty which perceives the existence of some right and of some wrong, whatever may be apprehended as such, and which refers actions to such right and wrong; the faculty which under all circumstances pronounces in favour of truth, and justice, and self-sacrifice, and courage, and purity, wherever these can be found, because it intuitively perceives their necessary excellence;—this faculty demands God. Conscience is unsatisfied, according to Kant, unless there exists some Being above the world, Who can hereafter reconcile the discrepancies which exist between virtue and fortune in this present life, in His quality of an arbiter of human conduct. Here Atheism, especially in its Positivist guise, pleads the disinterestedness of real virtue,

[1] Kritik der Reinen Vernunft, pp. 462-491, ed. Rosenkranz. Sämmtt. Werke, 2er Theil. These criticisms are discussed by Kleutgen, Theologie der Vorzeit. Bd. ii. p. 46, *sqq.* Philosophie der Vorzeit, ii. diss. 9, 1.

which is good and does good for the sake of goodness, seeking no reward, and daunted by no misfortune.[1] But when Kant maintains that there must be a moral God, he does this not in the interests of a mercenary virtue, but in those of an absolute and consummate justice, which proclaims in every human conscience the necessity of establishing an harmony or correspondence between the conditions of human existence on the one hand, and man's demerits or deserts on the other.

Thus it is that conscience demands God; and the atheistic whisper in the fool's heart of which the Psalmist speaks, belongs in truth to moral rather than to intellectual folly. It is ultimately traceable to a failure to perceive and feel the mighty and abiding contrast which exists between moral good and moral evil, and the necessary bearing of this contrast upon the ultimate destinies of the universe. In a good man, belief in God results from belief in the invincibility of good; the intensity or feebleness of a man's belief in God is a spiritual thermometer, whereby the temperature of his moral being may be pretty accurately measured. When the moral sensibilities are weakened or blunted by culpable indulgence until known sin is tolerable or even welcome, then the intellect is always open to theories which represent good and evil as alike forms of the Universal Life, or as equally fatal results of that "unreasoning and irresistible piece of machinery which we name

[1] Cf. too Strauss Glaubensl. 1, 393, qu. by Luthardt, Lect. III., whom I here follow.

the Universe." But although the human conscience is an earnest theistic apologist in exact proportion to its vitality, its affirmation of God should not be divorced from the intellectual inferences which the universe suggests to us. The evidential strength of Theism, like that of Christianity, lies not in any single proof, but in the collective force of the various evidences which are producible in its favour; and of these, the cry of conscience, if the strongest practically, is, after all, only one. Nor does it follow that because conscience is a true guide towards the throne of a Living and a Moral God, it is therefore an infallible judge in reviewing all that He may reveal to us about Himself or the laws of His government. We may reasonably accept the witness of the universal conscience of good men in favour of Theism, without binding ourselves to accept all that has been pleaded by individuals in the name of conscience against portions of the Jewish history, for example, or the doctrine of the Atonement. If it be urged from another side that it is after all "the conscience of fallen man upon which we rely for this great affirmation of God," the reply is, that the Fall cannot have destroyed our powers of apprehending truth, or it would have destroyed our responsibility, and that it is not the weakness which the Fall has wrought in human nature, but the strength which still survives it, whereby man affirms the existence of a Moral God and seeks Him. So far as man is a fallen being, no doubt, at the approach of the Lord God, he "hides himself amid the trees of the garden," to the end of time. But those truth-seeking elements of his spiritual nature which, as the Christian creed teaches, were in Paradise invigorated by a robe of supernatural grace, afterwards forfeited by the sin of our first parents, are throughout heathendom still kindled into activity by the prevenient grace of the Holy Spirit, breathing as He wills across the deserts; and thus fallen man seeks the Lord, if haply he might feel after Him and find Him, though He be not far from every one of us,[1] instinctively assured, as all good men must be, of His existence, and hoping that He may be fully unveiled at last.

Yet the feebleness of conscience in fallen man is a fact of significance. Although conscience seeks in God, not merely, as does intellect, a solution of the problem of the universe, but a Legislator Who has given and Who will enforce the law of right and wrong written in the human heart, conscience is nevertheless in the mass of men, if left to itself, too enfeebled to keep a Moral God clearly in view, even when it has caught sight of Him. It requires an aid external to itself, a token from its Object that it is not mistaken about Him. It requires a revelation. Without a revelation, historical theism is either the fruitless speculation of a few isolated thinkers, or the underlying idea of a popular superstition which obscures and degrades it. In a certain true sense it is itself a revelation; but its utterances require a countersign in the world without, which may make it certain that the inner legislator is also the Ruler of the Universe. Conscience itself, exactly in the

[1] Acts xvii. 27.

ratio of the clearness with which it discerns the moral nature of God, discerns the implied necessity of a revelation. It is sure that He Who is Himself just and merciful, cannot leave men altogether to themselves: that the All-Good cannot permanently disappoint the desires and powers which He has Himself implanted. And thus the antecedent probability of a revelation is to a good man not less than overwhelming; and Christianity assures us that his conviction is warranted by the fact.

The substance of the Christian revelation of God consists not merely in the teaching of Jesus Christ, together with the old Hebrew literature on which He sets His seal, and the apostolical doctrine which He warrants by anticipation, but also in His life. His life was an unveiling of God to the eye of man's sense, that the eye of man's spirit might understand Him. Christ's life, not less than His teaching, confirms the highest instincts of the human conscience, and educates them up to a point which of themselves they could never have reached. But how is man enabled to identify the Author of this law within him, perfectly reflected, as it is, in the Christ, with the Author of the law of the universe without him? The answer is, by miracle. Miracle is an innovation upon physical law,—or at least a suspension of some lower physical law by the intervention of a higher one,—in the interests of moral law. The historical fact that Jesus Christ rose from the dead identifies the Lord of physical life and death with the Legislator of the Sermon on the

Mount. Miracle is the certificate of identity between the Lord of Nature and the Lord of Conscience,—the proof that He is really a Moral Being Who subordinates physical to moral interests. Miracle is the meeting-point between intellect and the moral sense, because it announces the answer to the efforts and yearnings alike of the moral sense and the intellect; because it announces revelation. It may be asked whether miracle, in revealing God, is not subversive of the idea of God, Whom it reveals. Does it not postulate in Him two contradictory wills, the one whereby He enacts a permanent law, the other whereby He suspends it? And is not this irreconcileable with the highest views of His nature, as the Immutable, Who is what He is unchangeably, because what He is, is absolutely the best? No. For this is to apply to the Divine Mind a human standard of measurement. Succession is a law of human thoughts; because the mind of man is finite. If I resolve to spend each day for the next six months in a given way, and then, three months hence, determine that I will spend one particular day very differently, I am without doubt guilty of traversing my original and general intention by a second and particular intention which contradicts it. But with God, no such self-contradiction is possible; because in the Divine Mind there is no succession, whether of ideas or resolves. The Eternal Being sees the end in the beginning; He sees the exception together with the rule so simultaneously, that it is untrue to say that He anticipates it. It is a simple, indivisible act of will, whereby He everlastingly wills the rule together with the exception—the exception with the rule. With Him is "no variableness, neither shadow of turning."[1] The idea that God, in working a miracle, contradicts His own earlier purpose in giving to the physical world unchangeable laws, not merely betrays a conception of law as something independent of the free activity of God, but introduces into our conception of the Divine Mind the finite and human idea of succession in thought and will. Whereas, in truth, He, the Infinite, embraces, by one single act, present, past, and future, the general and the particular, the individual and the universal; reaching, as the Wise Man says, "from one end to another, mightily, and smoothly and sweetly ordering all things."[2]

But does God compromise His dignity by working a miracle, or by exerting a special Providence over His works? It is pleaded, indeed, that He must do so. It is said to be inconceivable that the Maker and Monarch of all these suns can interest Himself in the concerns of one of the smallest of His planets; in a particular race of creatures on its surface, in individual members of that race, in you and me. To imagine this, we are told, is only to indulge human self-love, which interprets all things, even the Deity Himself, by the promptings of its own boundless self-complacency.

And yet, what kind of "dignity" is it which is thus pleaded in order to depreciate the freedom, energy, and

[1] S. James i. 17. [2] Wisd. viii. 1.

ubiquity of God's Providential Rule? It is at best the dignity of an oriental despot; he is too engrossed in the cares of personal government, or in the pursuits of personal indulgence, to listen to the voices and to study the wants of the poor, who struggle and suffer around the walls of his seraglio. The notion that a really great intelligence will concern itself only and exclusively with broad principles and general interests, to the neglect of particulars and details, is, even when we are speaking of human minds, a mistaken notion. This vulgar contempt for details belongs to the pretentious imitation rather than to the reality of mental power. A really great intelligence combines the observation and study of details with the firm grasp of comprehensive principles; and in this power of combining things, which in lower minds are found apart, lies the strength and secret of its greatness. Nor is this less, rather it is much more the case, with the Eternal Mind. God is not less Divine in literally numbering the sparrows that fall to the ground, and the hairs of the human head, than in formulating the highest laws which govern either planetary systems or spiritual intelligences; while this comprehensive and penetrating interest and action, spending itself upon the whole outward and inward life of His creatures, is the symptom and expression of the moral interest which the reasonable creation commands in the heart of the Creator.

No; God's greatness is not enhanced by systems which would banish Him from the world, or condemn Him to impotence. The miracles of Christianity are so far from compromising its Theism, that they illustrate and secure it. The God of Christianity is no mere First Cause, or Supreme Intelligence. He is a Moral God. If He is Power and Wisdom, He is also Sanctity, Justice, Providence, Mercy, Love. According to the Gospel, Love is His Essence; and love is interest in, and self-sacrifice for that which is its object. It is such a God as this alone Who can be the adequate object of religion.

Traceable everywhere in human history, traceable especially in the history of one separated and chosen race, the interest of the Perfect Moral Being in the moral and thinking creatures of His hand culminates at Bethlehem and on Calvary. The Incarnation of the Eternal Son, the manifestation of the Divine life of Love, and Justice, and Compassion, and Purity, flashing through a veil of flesh, and leading up to a death of agony and shame, which alters the whole existing moral relation between earth and heaven; this is the glorious creed which rivets a Christian's conviction of the moral intensity of the life of God. "God so loved the world that He gave His only begotten Son." What could He do more in order to convince us that He is not merely a Force or an Intelligence, but a Heart? At the feet of Him who could say, "He that hath seen Me hath seen the Father," we understand, and feed upon the certainty, that God is moral as well as intellectual "light, and that in Him is no darkness at all." When a man's hold upon this creed is gone, his thought falls back, at best, upon the more rudimentary and less adequate ideas of the Godhead; the darker mysteries of the world's history present themselves with more painful force; and the mind tends inevitably, in the last resort, either to Deism or to Pantheism; to a Deism which just permits God to create, and then dismisses Him from His creation; or to a Pantheism which identifies Him with all the moral evil in the universe, and ends by propagating the worship of new Baals and Ashteroths.

A few words in conclusion.

God being really alive, His existence is a fact with which no other fact that the human mind can come to recognize will possibly compare. Nothing among created things that can engage and stimulate thought, nothing that can warm and expand affection, nothing that can invigorate will and purpose, ought, in the judgment of any thinking human being, to compete with the Eternal God. Our reasonable duty towards God is "to believe in Him, to fear Him, and to love Him, with all the heart, with all the mind, with all the soul, and with all the strength." And yet that unbegun, unending, self-existent Life; that boundless Intelligence administering a boundless Power; that long array of moral Attributes which win our love while they must also move our reverence and fear; what is He, our God, to us? Do we thirst for God? As the days, and months, and years pass, do we ever look out of and beyond ourselves upon that vast ocean of Uncreated Life Which encircles us, Which penetrates our inmost selves? Do we ever think steadily, so as to dwell with a real intellectual interest upon Him Who is the first and highest of truths, to Whose free bounty we ourselves owe the gift of existence, and to Whom we must one day account for our use of it? Do we ever sincerely desire to love Him, and to live for Him? Or are we constantly hurrying along our solitary path from one vanishing shape towards another, while we neglect the Alone Unchangeable? Be sure that, if we will, in God revealed in Christ, the soul may slake the thirst of the ages; and the dreariest, and darkest, and most restless existence may find illumination and peace. "This God is our God for ever and ever: He will be our guide unto death, and beyond it." To each one of us, now, He is, if we will; if we will, He will be, for ever, to each the Eternal Truth, wherein thought can never find its limit; the Uncreated Beauty, "most Ancient, yet always Fair," whereof affection can never tire; the Perfect Rule, existing eternally in the Life of the Necessary Moral Being, whereunto each created will may perpetually conform itself, yet never exhaust its task. Without this Awful and Blessed Being, man has no adequate object, even during these days of his brief earthly existence; his thought, his affection, his purpose spring up and are exercised only that they may presently waste and die. With God, the human soul not merely interprets the secret of the universe; it comprehends, and is at peace with, itself. For God is the satisfaction of its thirst;—He is the object of Religion.

LECTURE III.

Third Sunday in Lent.

THE SUBJECT OF RELIGION—THE SOUL.

Ps. viii. 4.

What is man, that Thou art mindful of him?

RELIGION, we have seen, is not a sentiment, or an idea, or even a code of moral practice. It involves the establishment and maintenance of a real bond between God on the one hand and man on the other. To the perfectness of this bond, feeling, thought, and moral earnestness on the part of man, contribute elements which are indispensable to it; so that religion in itself, although beyond each of them, is dependent upon all. Its object, as we have also seen, is the Personal and Moral God. In a mere first cause, in a mighty force, in an all-surveying intelligence, religion finds nothing to which it can attach itself; and systems which, like Pantheism, deny the personality of God, or, as did the old Deism, remove Him from all interest in and moral action upon the world, are thereby destructive of religion. And we have so far anticipated the matter before us, as to observe that, whatever else may be said for or against it, Christianity satisfies those conditions of a real religion, in which these theories severally fail; and that in Christendom, the purity and spirituality of a Personal God on the one hand, and His intimate contact with us men on the other, by means of a Personal Incarnation, are fully and equally recognized. But this brings us face to face with a question of scarcely inferior importance, at least from our human and practical point of view. Religion being a real relation between man and God, it is natural and inevitable to pass from considering one of its terms to the consideration of the other. If God be the object, what is the subject of religion? What is this created being who can thus enter into relations with the high majesty of heaven? or, as the Psalmist puts it at once more reverently and more truthfully, "What is man, that Thou art mindful of him?" What is it in man which makes him capable of this exceptional relation to God, as implied in his capacity for religion?

It would be a mistake to treat this inquiry on which we are embarking as so entirely speculative that it can secure or fortify no practical results. It is easy, but unwise, in days like ours to ignore the great questions which open beneath our feet as well as above our heads, under the pretence of being practical men who have neither time nor inclination for theory. No doubt, it is better to be a good man than to be a good psychologist; but an accurate notion of the real nature of the soul may contribute very materially in an age like ours to personal enthusiasm for practical goodness. How are you to decide whether man is capable of religion, or how far his capacity extends, until you know what, in his inmost, deepest being, man really is? In other words, this question of man's capacity for religion is substantially the question whether man be not merely a bodily organism, but also and especially a spiritual personality.

Certainly Revelation has familiarized Christians with the angels, as supramundane beings, in a very high degree capable of religion. But religion, as it comes before us on the surface of this planet, is a monopoly of man. Among the lower creatures we find nothing like it; we can discover no place for it. Man is the highest being of which these creatures have cognizance. Often, indeed, may we discover in their attachment to ourselves, in their fidelity, in their tenderness, in the true delicacy of the attention which they shew us, much that rebukes us when we reflect on the poor service that we ourselves pay to a Higher Master. But having no unseen world open to them, and being, as they are, incapable of any properly reflective thought, they are also incapable of religion, of any consciously personal relationship to the Source of all Life. But man can look above and beyond this world of sense; he can enter into real communion with the Monarch of both worlds; and the secret of his doing this lies in that which, by virtue of God's bountiful gift and appointment, he himself is as distinct from the creatures around him.

I.

What is man? What, let us ask, is this or that given man of our acquaintance, a near relation, one of ourselves? In the distance, or at first sight, a single human being is what the world chiefly associates with him; he is so much property, so much professional skill, so much political influence, so much social power, so much literary reputation, so much practical capacity for public affairs. Upon these things the public eye is wont to rest chiefly, if not exclusively; these things are labelled with this or that great name when it is repeated in conversation or in the newspapers. But they are only the accidents of any human life. They are external to it. They tell us nothing about it, nothing at least that a true appreciation of human greatness would most care to know. When do we see the man himself? We stand face to face with him; we listen to a voice; we note the peculiarities of a manner; we study the ever-varying lines of a human countenance; but we are still outside the real man. His voice, his manner, his expression, may tell us something about him; it may be a great deal; but they are not himself. We get nearer his real self, when we can observe and compare and take to pieces what he says and does; in his speech and his action, he reveals at least some portion of his character. But that which speaks and acts is beneath speech and action; it is always and necessarily invisible. The knife of no anatomist, however delicately wielded, can detect it in the folds of any human brain; no psychologist can draw it out into the light by an exhaustive analysis of any human thought. Underlying all the outward decorations of man's life; underlying the human face, and form, and speech, and action, although thrilling through them as if threatening ever and anon to become visible; underlying all that is most private and subtle even in secret thought, is that around which all else is gathered, and without which all else would be stripped of its significance, without which it would never have been or would cease to be.

What is man? He is, in the root and seat of his being, a person. He is that which each of us means when he says, "I." Let us turn to look at this question from within, rather than from without; for after all, it is within ourselves that we can, each for himself, only and really grapple with it. What do we mean, each of us, by "I." We mean, first of all, something distinct, utterly, profoundly distinct, from all that is not "I"; something which is conscious, as nothing else is concious, of this deep distinctness. I think, and I know that it is only I who think; I think about myself, and I know that it is myself only upon which I only am thinking; no other self commingles with this consciousness, or I should not be myself; I am thus conscious of my own identity, and of my radical separateness from all besides. Nay, more, I can trace and assert this identity of myself with myself, this separateness of myself from all that is not myself, for a long term of past years. When the outward circumstances of my life were far other than they are now; when my bodily mien was so different that none could recognize in it the myself of to-day; when the inner companions of my secret being were not as they have been since, so that I had other thoughts, other feelings, other resolves than now; yet still underlying these differences there was, deep down at bottom, the same self, thinking, feeling, resolving then, even as it resolves, and feels, and thinks now. And of no one fact am I more certain, or so certain, as of this;—that this self of the present is the self of thirty or forty years ago; that it was then as it is now, that it is now as it was then, a thing distinct from all else in the universe; and a thing of which, among creatures, I alone have actual cognizance. And as I am certain that it is separate from all besides, and that, as long as my memory will serve me, it has never been otherwise; so I feel at this moment, as I always have felt, that I possess it; that its thoughts are *my* thoughts; that its will is *my* will; that this thought and will are not powers which come in upon me like a flood and possess me, but that they are strictly forms of my own activity. If I think, I choose to think; if I will, it is I, and no other being in the universe, who does will; my will is the exercise of a freedom, unshared by any partner of my life; and, if I choose, indestructible.[1]

[1] See Psychologie, by Amedée Jacques, in the Manuel de Philosophie, Hachette, 1867. In Is. xxvi. 9, the *Ego* אֲנִי is clearly distinguished both from the נַפְשִׁי and the רוּחִי; in Prov. xxxiii. 15, and Eccles. vii. 25, it is distinguished from the לִבִּי of the Speaker. In Scripture *πρόσωπον* (2 Cor. i. 11) refers to external manifestation of the person, and *ὑπόστασις* (Heb. i.

Such, or, at least, something of this kind, is the sense of personality as we, each one of us, experience it. As long as we can remember, it has been at the bottom of all that we have felt, thought, and done; it has penetrated every movement of our minds and hearts; it has welded the many elements of our lives, outward and inward, moral and intellectual, spiritual and even bodily, into a consistent whole. When it is felt, our inmost being is felt; we can get no deeper than that reflective thought, than that conscious will. Here we touch, so far as we can touch, personal spirit; and it is because man is a personal spirit, or, as Scripture terms it, a being made in the image of God, that he is master of the world around him.[1] The mere animal is not thus conscious of, and capable of reflecting, on his own existence. He lives and feels; he carries instinct forward, it may be, to the very confines of reason. But he does not comprehend his life; he does not reflect that it is he who lives; he is not conscious of remembering a line of personal existence, unshared by any other being, and threading a series of years and a long train of divergent circumstances. He does not anticipate a future.

3, xi. 1) to the substance that underlies the appearance. There is no word in Scripture to express "person" in the sense of a self-conscious, self-determining being. Del. Bibl. Psychologie, vi. 1. Wörter's art. Seele in Wetzer and Wette; Dict. Encycl.

[1] On the Likeness of God in man see Delitzsch, Biblische Psychologie, ii., § 2. The Divine Image consists in man's self-consciousness and moral freedom, *τὸ νοερὸν καὶ αὐτεξούσιον*. Man's dominion over the earthly world is "an effluence of the Divine likeness, and not the Divine likeness itself." By means of the Resurrection even man's body attains *τὴν εἰκόνα τοῦ ἐπουρανίου* (1 Cor. xv. 49), in that it is transfigured into the image of the God-man. See the whole of this interesting section.

Neither is he free or deliberate in his exercise of will: his will is only impulsive desire or passion, unregulated by intelligence; it is not his instrument; it is his master. Being thus the slave of nature around him and of his own nature, of his own instincts, and of the force of circumstance, he never can project himself beyond nature, and so rise above it, and take the measure of it and of his own relation towards it. He is thus passive when face to face with his nature, he is thus entirely under its control, because he altogether belongs to it; because in him there is nothing which comes from a higher world, and is independent of the world of sense.[1] Accordingly the single animal is only a specimen of his kind, the individual exists only in the species: but man, besides belonging on his animal side to an animal species, yet knows himself to be, in his individual capacity, a solitary essence, personal and indivisible. With man, the animal species, the lower nature which he shares with his kind, is subordinate to the individual, because in man that which constitutes the individual, his inmost being, belongs to a separate and a higher order of existence.[2]

[1] Wörter, art. Seele, ubi. sup.

[2] It were to be wished, observes Delitzsch, that personality and individuality were less frequently confused in common language than they are. Personality is common to all men as such: by it men are raised above plants and beasts. Between the "thought," feeling, instinct of the brute, and the inner life of man, who is conscious of himself, and can in thought project himself beyond himself, there is an impassable gulf. Individuality only marks off the single specimen of the kind, whether it be man or beast; it implies nothing as to his subjective life. Although this obvious distinction is not formally expressed in Scripture, it is observable that in the narrative of the creation מִין is used only of plants and beasts, not of man; as if

This consciousness of personal life is not to be referred to anything in man's physical constitution. Thought after all is not merely phosphorus; and psychology is not correctly described as a branch of physiology. The great Scottish thinkers of half a century ago laid much stress upon the doctrine of what they called "internal facts." By an internal fact they did not mean a fact removed from the cognizance of the five senses; because there are many purely physiological facts which might be defined in this way,—as, for example, valvular action in the circulation of the blood. They meant an act of which the personal consciousness alone takes cognizance. If you lift a heavy weight, so far as the visible muscular exertion of the arm goes, that is an external fact; but the cause of this external fact is an internal fact, a determination of your will—that is, of yourself; and of this cause you alone are conscious. How your will acts upon your muscles, you cannot say; but this at least you do know, that it is your will which, by a voluntary self-determination, caused the movement of the muscles of your arm: and this internal fact is just as certain to you as the external one. Or suppose that you feel annoyance at some action of a neighbour, and reflect almost immediately that this feeling is undeserved, and fall back upon this and that considera-tion in order to set it aside, and succeed in doing so. Here you have three distinct internal facts; the original

to imply that man is more than an individual specimen of a kind,—that he is a person.—Bibl. Psych. iv. 1.

feeling, the bringing reason to bear upon that feeling, and the altered state of feeling which succeeds. All of these are strictly internal, strictly peculiar to the consciousness; yet as appreciable by observation, and as immediately appreciable, as any fact of physiology. There is no necessity, exclaims the eminent thinker who suggests this illustration, for losing ourselves "in metaphysical hypotheses, in order to demonstrate the spirituality of the soul, and Kant was right in throwing these old-fashioned arguments to the winds. The spirituality of the soul is a fact; it is a positive fact; it is a fact just as notorious as the sunlight. Men are still inquiring, and will probably inquire while time shall last, what matter is. But we do practically know what spirit is, for we have each one of us a sample of it in ourselves, that is to say, in the thinking, feeling, determining subject which we name 'self.'"[1]

It would be an impertinence to say that the spirituality of the human soul "is taught in Scripture," because Holy Scripture everywhere presupposes it, and is unintelligible without it. But a question may be raised as to the form in which it is taught there. Scripture sometimes appears to exhibit human nature as composed of two elements, sometimes as of three. Moses represents man as originating from "the combination of an immediate breathing of God with an earthly body,"[2] and Solomon distinguishes

[1] Saisset, L'âme et la Vie, pp. 16, 17, 18, 22.
[2] Gen. ii. 7; cf. Del. Bibl. Psych. ii. § 4.

the dust which at death must "return to the earth as it was" from "the spirit" that "shall return unto God who gave it."[1] After a like manner our Lord distinguishes the true life or soul of man[2] from his animal life, and the "spirit," which in His disciples was "willing," from the "flesh" that was weak;[3] and in dying He resigns His Human Soul to the Father, with the words, "Into Thy hands I commend My Spirit."[4] In the same manner S. Paul bids Christians glorify God both in their body and in their spirits, since both body and spirit belong to Him;[5] and S. James compares faith without works to that separation between the body and the spirit which implies the death of the body.[6] In these passages, man is regarded as composed of a body and of a single supersensuous nature, which is sometimes called life or soul,[7] and sometimes spirit; but elsewhere, this immaterial nature itself is subdivided into self-conscious, self-determining spirit, and animal life-power or soul. Thus S. Paul prays that the spirit, and soul, and body of the Thessalonian Christians, each part subsisting in its perfect integrity, may be preserved blameless until our Lord's second

[1] Eccles. xii. 7. [2] S. Matt. vi. 25, οὐχὶ ἡ ψυχὴ πλεῖόν ἐστι τῆς τροφῆς.
[3] S. Matt. xxvi. 41. [4] S. Luke xxiii. 46.
[5] 1 Cor. vi. 20, see text. [6] S. James ii. 26.
[7] "According to the *usus loquendi* of all the books of the Bible, נֶפֶשׁ ψυχή, frequently denotes the entire inward nature of man." This is true even of S. Paul. If ψυχή in his writings means nothing more than "vis quâ corpus viget et movetur," he is at issue with S. Luke, with the Epistle to the Hebrews, and with Eph. vi. 6, Col. iii. 23, Phil. i. 27; in all of which passages the seat of moral resolve is placed in the ψυχή. Cf. Delitzsch, Bibl. Psych. iii. § 9.

coming;[1] and the word of God is described in the Epistle to the Hebrews as having, from its moral power, an analytical efficacy which separates as clearly between the spiritual and psychical elements of man's immaterial nature, as between the life of sensation and the life of motion in his corporeal nature.[2] Still it cannot be concluded from these two passages that man consists of three essentially distinct elements. If this language of S. Paul obliges us to see in soul and spirit something more than two distinct relations of man's inward nature, it does not imply more than two distinct departments of that nature, the higher region of self-conscious spirit and self-determining will, which belongs to man as man; and the lower region of appetite, perception, imagination, memory, which in the main is common to the undying soul of man and the perishable inmost being of the brute. Man's soul is not a third nature, poised between his spirit and his body; nor yet is it a sublimate of his bodily organization, any more than his body is a precipitate of his soul. It is the outer clothing of the spirit, one with it in essence, yet distinct in functions; the centre of man's life, psychical and animal, is his spirit.[3]

But whatever Holy Scripture may explicitly say about

[1] 1 Thess. v. 23, *ὁλόκληρον ὑμῶν τὸ πνεῦμα, καὶ ἡ ψυχὴ, καὶ τὸ σῶμα.*

[2] Heb. iv. 12, *διϊκνούμενος ἄχρι μερισμοῦ ψυχῆς τε καὶ πνεύματος, ἁρμῶν τε καὶ μυελῶν.*

[3] In our own day Anton Günther revived the psychological dualism of Occam, by making the distinction between the soul and spirit in man an essential distinction; in other words, by representing each man as possessed of two souls, one the seat of reason, the other of sensation and growth.

the spiritual personality of man as a formal doctrine, it implies much more by its constant appeal to man's higher nature. From first to last it treats man as a being who, although clothed in an animal form, is essentially and in himself a spirit. It surrounds him with precepts which a self-determining spirit only can obey; with examples, of which only a reflecting spirit can enter into the force and drift; with prayers, aspirations, modes of thought and feeling, that have no meaning for a being who is not experimentally conscious of his spiritual subsistence. Especially is this observable in those Divine pages which form the inmost sanctuary of Holy Scripture; in the Life and Words of our Lord Jesus Christ. As human forms pass before Him, in the Gospel, although He is constantly relieving human want and pain, it is plain that the outward man means for Him, relatively, almost nothing, and that His eye rests persistently, exclusively, upon the man within. As we accompany Him in that brief but exhaustive study of humanity, we feel before the centurion or Pilate little or nothing of the majesty of the Roman name. Although Christ appeared when the Empire of the Cæsars was in its splendour, He speaks of the "kings of the Gentiles," in a phrase of studied vagueness; as if to suggest the utter insignificance of the highest political interests which only touch man's outward life, when they are contrasted with those higher in-

That this theory has no biblical warrant appears to have been satisfactorily shewn by Delitzsch: its experimental difficulties are obvious. The *Ego* which thinks, reasons, wills, is, we all of us know, identical with the *Ego* which experiences the sensations of sight, smell, hearing, touch.

terests of the human spirit which He had come to promote. Even the greatness and authority of the successors of Aaron disappears, or recedes into the background, in the atmosphere of this exacting estimate, which knows no respect of persons; while on the other hand, at His bidding, a few obscure and illiterate Galilean peasants become respectively a S. Peter, a S. John, a S. Mary Magdalen—names which of themselves recall neither political weight nor intellectual prestige, but types of spiritual character, beautiful and majestic, upon which already eighteen centuries of progressive civilization have been forward to lavish all but the best of their reverence and their love.

It is indeed as personal spirits, tabernacling in bodily forms, that we men are capable of religion. Resolve man's higher nature into physiological sensation with Materialism, and religion becomes an absurdity. As spirits, we are linked and bound to the Father of Spirits; as spirits, we believe, we hope, we love; as spirits, we enter into the complex mystery and activities of prayer; as spirits, we take in each other that deep and penetrating interest which pierces beneath the outline of the human animal, and holds true converse with the supersensuous being within. All that weakens or lowers our consciousness of being spirits, weakens in that proportion our capacity for religion: all that enhances that consciousness, as surely enlarges it.

II.

Man, then, if we track him to the centre of his being, is a spirit, whatever be the dignity and organic indispensableness of his outward form. What do we know about the origin of man's spirit, of his deepest self? We know when and under what conditions a human body comes into existence. What do we know about the origin of a human soul?

If we take account of the ancient and of the Eastern world, one of the most popular answers to this question will be found in the theory that the soul exists before the body. Sometimes this is stated without an attempt at closer definition; more frequently it takes the form of a doctrine of Metempsychosis. According to this doctrine the spiritual part of each man's being is as a forced emigrant, who has previously occupied other frames, and who may have others to inhabit hereafter; although man's inextinguishable hope suggests that an escape from this fatal cycle may be achieved by pre-eminent virtue, which will at length secure an incorporeal immortality for the weary wanderer.[1]

The Western and less systematized form of the doctrine is due to Plato. Plato, who did so much in the way of training the ancient world to realize the greatness and uniqueness of the soul, accounted for the soul's present

[1] For a recent European theory of a curiously Gnostic complexion, see "Le Lendemain de la Mort, ou la vie future selon la Science," par Louis Figuier. Paris, 1871.

and, as he deemed it, humiliating relation to the body, by saying that the soul had existed previously in another state of being, and was condemned to tenant a human frame as a kind of punishment. Plato was probably less anxious to give a complete account of the origin of the soul, than to explain the source of certain ideas which he encountered in the human mind. They occupied much of his attention, and he desired to invest them with an authority that might place them beyond the reach of popular discussion. To Plato it seemed that these ideas were relics of a higher knowledge enjoyed by the soul in some earlier stage of its existence; he could account for them no otherwise, because they so transcended the poor realities of man's present experience. Thoughts which appeared to result from scientific speculation were in truth only a form of memory—memory of some bygone existence, passed in an ideal world from which the soul had fallen down into the sphere of sense and under conditions of time.[1]

Plato's speculation about the soul was of deeper and more permanent interest to humanity at large, than the particular theory which led him to adopt it. It naturally found its way, in company with his other guesses, to Alexandria. It was adopted by Neo-Platonist thinkers, and even in the Jewish schools; it was taught by Philo, as well as by Plotinus; it was filtered through Essenism into the religious philosophy of the Talmud and the Cabbala;[2]

[1] *ἡμῖν ἡ μάθησις οὐκ ἄλλο τι ἢ ἀνάμνησις τυγχάνει οὖσα.* Cf. Plat. Phæd., E. 73-77, 246.

[2] Delitzsch quotes Joel, Religions philosophie der Sohar, pp. 107-109.

it entered into more than one type of Gnosticism; it appears among the other eccentricities of the eccentric Origen; it forms a link between the philosophical bishop of Cyrene, Synesius, and the outer world of Pagan thought. But it was stoutly opposed by the immense majority of Christian teachers,[1] and was finally condemned by the collective Church, as an untenable error.[2] For it never had any basis in Holy Scripture; not even in those writings which are historically connected with Alexandrian thought, or which have been supposed, on strictly internal grounds, to have an Alexandrian colouring.[3] To suppose that it underlies the doctrine of an original or birth-sin, as taught in the New Testament, is to forget that the great teacher of that doctrine expressly states that the consequences of the first sin devolve upon those who have not sinned after the similitude of Adam's transgression.[4]

1 Even by Clement of Alexandria, *ὁ Θεὸς ἡμᾶς ἐποίησεν οὐ πρόοντας· ἔχρην γὰρ καὶ εἰδέναι ἡμᾶς ὅπου ἦμεν εἰ προ ἦμεν.* Qu. by Klee, Dogmatik. p. 433, from Strom. viii.; Maii, tom. vii. p. 88. S. Peter of Alexandria characterises it as a shred of heathenism: *τὸ γὰρ μάθημα τοῦτο τῆς ἑλληνικῆς ἐστι φιλοσοφίας κένης καὶ ἀλλοτρίας οὔσης τῶν ἐν Χριστῷ εὐσεβῶς θελόντων ζῆν.* De Anim. frag., *ib.*

2 In the Second Council of Constantinople; Hefele, Conciliengesch. ii. 772.

3 *E.g.*, not in Wisd. viii. 19, 20, which refers to an altogether exceptional attribute or Personality. The Cabbalist reference to Eccles. xii. 7, and Origen's to Rom. ix. 11-13, Luke i. 47, Jerem. i. 5, are set aside on examining the passages. Nor are such arguments as Heb. vii. 9 to the point. The pre-existence of our Lord's Divine Person, as taught in S. John and S. Paul, would be relevant, if those Apostles had taught the pre-existence of any one else, and if, in His case, this pre-existence did not clearly attach to a representation of His Personal Dignity as superhuman. His Human Soul was, like His Body, created in time, and then hypostatically united to His Pre-existent Godhead.

4 Rom. v. 14, *ἐπὶ τοὺς μὴ ἁμαρτήσαντας ἐπὶ τῷ ὁμοιώματι τῆς παραβάσεως Ἀδὰμ.*

The conception of a pre-existing soul is, moreover, broadly at issue with the Scriptural account of man's creation. Holy Scripture knows of no creation of souls prior to the creation of bodies; the creation of the first man comprises the simultaneous creation of his body and his soul. Scripture carries us up to no moral act of any soul living and working before the creation of Adam's body; it traces no moral circumstance of man's present condition higher than to the sin of Adam in Paradise. It represents marriage as honourable, and the offspring of marriage as a blessing from the Lord; but these representations would ill consist with the theory which would treat the human body, the product of marriage, as only a strange house of detention, wherein the unwilling soul is bound during a lifetime, far from its true end and home. In short, the theory of the soul's pre-existence is broadly at issue with the biblical and Christian doctrine of man, which makes man the synthesis of body and spirit; since, according to that theory, man existed in his completeness, as spirit, before he was sent to inhabit a human frame. And in this way such a theory cuts up by the roots that profound argument for the future resurrection of the body, which is suggested by the fact that the body is, under the terms of man's natural constitution, the soul's one adequate organ and instrument; it reduces the body to the rank of a temporarily indwelt shell, which might be escaped from with advantage. Nor is the verdict of our experience at issue with that of Christian doctrine in this particular. If we have all of us existed in some previous state of being, how is it that no living memory records any one distinct event in this presumed phase of past existence? If all traces of this supposed pre-existent life should have been blotted out from one memory, or from the majority of memories, how are we to explain their entire disappearance from all? Such universal oblivion of a great past is in fact inexplicable, except upon the extreme and violent hypothesis of a miraculous annihilation of memory in all spirits that have been heretofore united to human forms. The failure of any one memory to recall the supposed life of human souls in another sphere of being, is as unfavourable to the supposition at the bar of reason, as its other demerits must be held to be condemnatory of it in the judgment of faith.[1]

But if man's soul cannot be supposed to exist, as an independent being, before the formation of his body, is it a part, the highest part, of that transmitted inheritance of life, which we receive, each one of us, from our earthly parents? Among the ancients this position was maintained most earnestly by Tertullian.[2] He had already broken away from the Church, and he wanted a strong psychological tenet capable of bearing him well out in the

[1] For some considerations to the contrary, see Delitzsch, Bibl. Psych. i. 1, who, however, insists that the theory in question has no Scriptural foundation.

[2] Cf. Tertull. de Animâ, c. 19. He speaks of the human soul "velut sarculus quidam ex matrice Adam in propaginem deducta;" and argues that in the process of natural conception, "cum omni suâ paraturâ pullulabit, tam intellectu quam sensu." Cf. passim, 19-21, 25-27, 37.

vigorous resistance which, in his Montanist isolation, he offered to the Marcionite notion of a pre-existing soul. Of course, if the soul was generated simultaneously with the body, there was no room left for saying that it had ever existed independently; and Tertullian accordingly pressed the theory of Traducianism, as it is termed, with this object, just as in a later age S. Augustine was attracted towards it, for another reason equally independent of its intrinsic merits.[1] If the soul was transmitted from sire to son, then it was easy to answer the Pelagian question, how original sin could be passed on together with it from Adam to his descendants. But, notwithstanding this powerful motive for accepting it, Augustine saw in the Traducianist doctrine an element of Materialism.[2] The ordinary comparison of lighting one lamp from the flame of another, was too gross an image accurately to adumbrate the act of giving being to an immaterial consciousness. The idea of the soul which Traducianism suggests, is really derived from animal analogies, and is inapplicable to the conception of a purely spiritual and indivisible essence. The difficulty was not removed by saying that the body was not, as in the theory

[1] Beausobre (Hist. Crit. de Manichée, Amst., 1734) goes so far as to attribute a strictly Traducianist doctrine respecting the origin of the soul to S. Augustine. How keenly Augustine felt the dangers of Materialism latent in this theory appears from such passages as De Gen. ad Litt. lib. x. cap. i. 24-25. His general language is studiously undecided: cf. De Animâ et ejus orig. i. 2; iv. 2. De Lib. Arbitr. iii. c. 21, n. 59. His hesitation is the more remarkable, as Pelagius made great use of Creatianism in opposing the Catholic doctrine of original sin. See his Letter to S. Jerome; Ep. 166, c. 5, 9.

[2] Ep. 190, ad Opt. c. iv. n. 13, 14, 15, qu. by Wörter.

of Tertullian, the real generating agent, but only one intermediate link in the process by which a soul is engendered by parent souls. When Lactantius asked whether, on the Traducianist hypothesis, the soul of an infant was to be supposed to be derived from the father, or from the mother, or from both parents at once, he asked a question which was, in fact, fatal to the theory.[1] It was inconceivable that a spirit, personal and indivisible, or that two spirits, should engender another spirit; because to conceive this was to attribute a purely animal process of propagation to denizens of the supersensuous world.[2] It has been observed that children generally resemble their parents in those qualities which we describe collectively as tempera-

[1] De opificio Dei, c. 19. Illud quoque venire in quæstionem potest: utrumne anima ex patre, an potiùs ex matre, an verò ex utroque generetur. Sed ego id meo jure ab ancipiti vindico. Nihil enim ex his tribus verum est, quia neque ex utroque neque ex alterutro seruntur animæ corporibus. Corpus enim ex corporibus nasci potest, quoniam confertur aliquid ex utroque; de animis anima non potest, quia *ex re tenui et incomprehensibili nihil potest decedere.*

[2] Delitzsch's attack upon the position that "the assumed ability of spirit to propagate itself is contrary to the dualism of nature and spirit," does not appear to be convincing. The Divine Nature being the Parent of the material as well as of the Spiritual Universe, those Eternal Truths internal to It, which are shadowed out by the Names of Father, and Son, may well be the archetypes of material rather than of spiritual facts in the universe. The Eternal Spirit Himself is "not begotten but proceeding." The חוֹלָלְתִּי of Prov. viii. 24, is to be referred to the Son, who is identical with the Wisdom of the Proverbs. The application of the metaphor of generation and birth to God's natural (Job xxxviii. 28; Ps. xc. 2; Deut. xxxii. 18) and supernatural (1 Pet. i. 3; James i. 18; 1 S. John iii. 9) creations does not warrant any inference as to a possible parental relationship between one created spirit and another. The angelic reference in Gen. vi. 1-4 is, to say the least, far too doubtful to be made the basis of an argument. But cf. Bibl. Psych. ii. § 7, sub fin.

ment, as belonging to the region of animal life-power; but that no such resemblance can be calculated on, or, where it does occur, regarded as other than purely accidental, in respect of strictly personal qualities, such as genius, or will.[1] Traducianism can undoubtedly point to great names who favour it in ancient and modern times;[2] and it rests on too large an area of possibilities to be rejected with anything like peremptoriness. But the general sense of the Church is now, as it has been in past times, against it; it does not seem to harmonize, at least naturally and easily, with the fixed outlines of a consistently spiritualist philosophy, or, notwithstanding the easy explanation which it affords of a doctrine of transmitted sin, to make itself really at home with such an estimate of man's spiritual nature as is implied by the great doctrines of the Christian creed.

The other and more generally received doctrine, is known as Creatianism. Each soul is an immediate work of the Creator: He is perpetually creating souls out of nothing, and infusing them into bodies.[3] He creates each soul at the moment when the body which is destined for it enters

[1] As by Wörter, ubi supra.

[2] S. Jerome, indeed, himself an earnest Creatianist, attributes Traducianism to the majority of Western teachers in his day: maxima pars occidentalium, Ep. 78, ad Marcell; but in antiquity Tertullian stands out almost alone in his unfaltering decision. Augustine hesitates. Of modern Traducianists, Delitzsch among Lutheran, and Klee among Roman Catholic writers, are perhaps the greatest.

[3] Quotidiè Deus operatur animas et in corpora mittit nascentium. S. Jerome; adv. Ruf. Apol. xvi. 1, 3. Traducianism he thinks absurd: Satis ridendi qui putant animas cum corporibus seri et non a Deo, sed a corporum parentibus generari. Qu. by Klee, Dogm.

really and properly on its inheritance of life.[1] Creatianism recognizes that sense of the immateriality of the human spirit which expressed itself falsely in the doctrine of a pre-existence, and which is so seriously compromised by Traducianism. Personal spirit, it is asserted by the Creatianist, cannot be transmitted from one created life to another, like animal vitality. Yet Creatianism recognizes the truth for which the Traducianists contended against the advocates of the soul's pre-existence, when it maintains that the soul and body are strictly contemporaneous in their origin, and that they have profound and ineffaceable relations to each other.

When it is pleaded against this theory of the origin of the soul that it is at issue with the Scriptural representation of a Sabbath rest, which brought God's creative activity to a close,[2] it is sufficient to reply that such an interpretation of the Mosaic narrative would oblige us to close our eyes to the proved fact of a later origin of new species of animals, besides being inconsistent with any adequate idea of God's providential relation to the world.[3] When it is said that Creatianism, if true, would enslave God, by bidding Him give existence to an immortal spirit at the will of the adulterer, and in defiance of His own law, this objection[4] does indeed reveal the peculiar malignity of sins against

[1] This is apparently the drift of Peter Lombard's often-quoted maxim: Creando infundit animas Deus et infundendo creat.

[2] As by Klee, Dogmatik, p. 431.

[3] S. John v. 17.

[4] S. Augustine admits to S. Jerome that, before hearing his answer to this difficulty, he had himself solved it by dwelling on God's power and will

marriage; but it is merely an extreme illustration of the general truth, that man can only sin with God's assistance; that all sin consists in the employment of God's bounty against Himself. When, lastly, it is urged that the transmission of original sin is on this hypothesis unintelligible, it may be sufficient to say that original sin, being rather of the nature of a defect than of a positive taint, there is no difficulty in understanding how created souls did not receive a gift which had been withdrawn from the race to which at birth they became united. Upon the whole, the Creatianist theory seems better to fall in with the scattered hints and with the general language of Scripture. It is apparently more in harmony with the account of the creation of man, and with the general representations of God's creative relationship to the spirit of man, which we find in the Old Testament.[1] Especially does it seem to be borne out by the distinction which is drawn in the Epistle to the Hebrews between the "fathers of our flesh" and the "Father of spirits."[2] These expressions discriminate with an accuracy from which there would seem to be no escape between the contribution made to the composite being of man by our heavenly

to draw good out of evil in all His earthly providences. The giving being to a soul, capable of knowing and loving its Creator, is of itself a good, however it may be occasioned. Ep. ad Hieron. 166, c. 5.

[1] Gen. ii. 7; Job xxxiii. 4; Ps. cxix. 73; Zech. xii. 1.

[2] Heb. xii. 9. The contrast, Delitzsch admits, between *τῆς σαρκὸς ἡμῶν πατέρες*, and the Divine *πατὴρ τῶν πνευμάτων*, is physical and not ethical. "There can hardly," he remarks, "be a more classical proof-text for Creatianism." The passages which imply the organic oneness and responsibility of the race of Israel do not set this aside (vii. 5, 10.) Cf. Num. xvi. 22.

Parent immediately, and that which He bestows through created channels of the gift of life.[1]

This question of the soul's origin has carried us into a region where we have at best to deal with high probabilities; where revelation has rather hinted at the truth than unveiled it, and where reason certainly cannot pretend to dogmatize. But it is not altogether unfruitful to look at this side of our subject, even where certainty is unattainable. To do so makes us all the more thankful for certainty, when we know that it is within our reach. After all, the difference between the Creatianists and Traducianists does not raise the question whether the human soul is made by God, but only the question whether it is immediately created by Him. All that we are and have, except the evil which we have wrought, and which clings to us, comes from the One Source of Life; but if religion finds its strength in this general conviction, it is especially stimulated by the belief that the soul is God's immediate handiwork. The belief that the inmost being of each one of us is created as immediately by God as was that of our first parent Adam, brings each of us into a felt relationship with God, and reminds us of our obligations towards Him, more effectively than would be the case if we supposed ourselves to receive spiritual as well as corporeal life through a long series of ancestors. It is this persuasion which underlies Bishop Andrewes' favourite ejaculatory

[1] Cf. Delitzsch's Discussion of Heb. xii. 9 against Elvard's theory that σάρξ means here the natural life in opposition to the regenerate life, Hebraerbr. in loc.

prayer from the Psalter, "Despise not Thou the work of Thine own Hands." It is not in the anatomy and faculties of the body, it is in the analysis and study of the soul, that the greatness of human life is best realized, and our indebtedness towards its Giver most deeply felt. This reflective reason; this heart, capable of a boundless expansion; this will, which may be trained to a freedom and an intensity of extraordinary power;—of what are these faculties so suggestive as of the knowledge, love, and service due to that Being of Beings Who is the End, as He is the Author, of this centre of complex and self-controlling life?

III.

Man, then, is a spirit; and, as it would seem, he is, as such, immediately created by God. The gravest question yet remains: What is his destiny? Whatever may be said of the importance of questions bearing on the soul's origin, no reflecting man will deny the interest of all that bears upon its future. It is true that even this question is ostentatiously set aside on the ground of its being unpractical to discuss it. "The dead," it is argued, "do not return to tell us their experience. What then can be known certainly of that which befalls them? We may hope, or we may conjecture; we may desire, or despair; we may dogmatize in the air, and make creeds of our aspirations; but would it not be better to confine ourselves to subjects that are well within the range of our experience, and where sure results are attainable, than to waste time and sympathy upon that which belongs really and only to the realm of fancy?"

This way of treating the subject is possible and not uncommon among young men and women in good health, who have never known a heartache; and in the pages of clever serials, where readers are carried forward almost unresistingly, by clear type and well-turned sentences, over the dreary wastes of sceptical thought. But the question of the eternal future is too pressing to be thus left at a distance, permanently. If religion has many enemies in the predominant tendencies of the modern world, she certainly has steady and inalienable allies in the permanent circumstances of human nature. To the most refined and cultured of ourselves, death is just as certain a contingency as it was to our rudest forefathers, and its dread solemnities enter just as penetratingly into the homes of rank and science, as into the humblest cottages in the land. Sooner or later it comes close to all of us, and the mists which hide its stern realities from our eyes roll away, and leave us face to face with them.

"They think that their houses shall continue for ever: and that their dwelling-places shall endure from one generation to another; and call the lands after their own names.

"Nevertheless man will not abide in honour: seeing that he may be compared unto the beasts that perish; this is the way of them.

. . . .

"They lie in the hell like sheep, death gnaweth upon them, and the righteous shall have domination over them in the morning: their beauty shall consume in the sepulchre out of their dwelling.

. . . .

"Be not thou afraid, though one be made rich: or if the glory of his house be increased;

"For he shall carry nothing away with him when he dieth: neither shall his pomp follow him.

"For while he lived he counted himself an happy man: and so long as thou doest well unto thyself, men will speak good of thee.

"He shall follow the generation of his fathers: and shall never see light.

"Man being in honour hath no understanding: but is compared unto the beasts that perish."[1]

This is the solemn irony of life, and from year to year we find ourselves face to face with it. Death does not move us much, when it visits those whom we do not know, or whom we know only slightly; when it only meets us as it wends its way gloomily through the crowded thoroughfare towards the distant cemetery, or as it catches our eye in the supplement of our daily newspaper. It

[1] Psalm xlix. 11, 12, 14, 16–20.

does not touch us as being what it is, so long as it only produces social changes which excite our interest, while it keeps sufficiently at a distance not to wound our hearts. We drape it in phrases which treat it as a solemn abstraction. No doubt it is solemn; but so is the war lately raging in Paraguay, or a Russian campaign in Central Asia. We should speak very differently of a revolutionary struggle in the streets of London, upon the issue of which it was clearly understood that our own life and property might immediately depend. But we find that at last death comes home to us, even to us, in all the closeness of its dreadful embrace. Not, it may be, this time to ourselves: that were perhaps more bearable. The one human being whom we have loved best on earth—the parent, the husband, the wife, the child—lies before us. We see what is coming. It is very gradual, perhaps, and there are many rallies in which vital power struggles with disease, in which hope flickers up in its contest with the presentiments of reason, only to die back into a deeper despair. It is very gradual —a slow processional movement to the grave: but the end comes at last. At last a day comes to which the preceding days are as if they had not been; a day comes which lives in memory. We can no longer reckon on hours; we dare not be away even for a few minutes, lest we should be too late. A change has taken place, which they know well who are familiar with death, and of which none can mistake the import. We feel, all feel, that the time is short, and a few words are said into which is compressed a life—

its most sincere thought and love—a few assurances, messages, entreaties; no more is possible. Already, one by one, the vital powers take their leave: first speech, then movement, then hearing, then even eyesight. Still there is breathing, now rapid and deep, now weaker and intermittent; and then there comes a last breath; and we wait; and there is none after it.

It lies before us, that loved form: only an hour ago it spoke: we speak to it now, but in vain. We bend over it in our agony, as if it was still what it had been; but we know—what would we not give to escape from our conviction?—that neither thought nor feeling tenants it now. And the question must rise then, if it never rose before, with an urgency proportioned to the grief which asks it;—Is all really over? Has the real being, which one short hour ago thought and felt so keenly, actually and for ever ceased to be?

Do you say that in presence of that passionate agony it is folly to ask for a decision which should only be dictated by the coolest, the calmest, the most unimpassioned, the most disinterested science? I answer that that agony, if it be not itself an argument, is well fitted to win a hearing for arguments to which, under ordinary circumstances, our materialistic science is deaf. Such a condition of feeling may be impatient on the one hand of a physiology which seeks for the immaterial spirit in the brain; as it cannot, on the other, enter into a metaphysical discussion of the alleged indestructibility of uncompounded essences. But being itself pain, mental pain, one of the great chastening, illuminating powers of the moral world, it is at least in a mood to understand a moral argument. And the moral argument for our immortality is, after all, the strongest of those upon which reason can fall back. It is no fancy which insists that Eternal Justice cannot close His account with any human conscience at the moment of death; that there must be an after-world in which the too unequal balance of suffering and happiness, of good and evil doing during life, will be surely rectified. We must do stern violence to the best and deepest instincts of our better nature before the voice of this argument can be silenced. It is a moral conviction which protests against the Materialistic theory that the soul is but an animated vapour which becomes extinct with the life of the bodily frame. It equally rejects the Pantheistic dream, that what looks like a separate personality ceases when we cease to breathe, while the soul sinks back into the vast under-current of boundless life, which is the fabled vital force of the Pantheistic universe. If morality has any serious basis in the nature of things, if it be not a dream or a conventionalism, there must be a future wherein each personal spirit will subsist under conditions which will have direct reference to its moral and spiritual attainments here.

For if one thing is evident to a man who takes notes of what passes within him with the lapse of time, it is that the inward being which he contemplates as "self," is continually developing. As the years pass, whether for good or evil, this immaterial, thinking, resolving being acquires accumulating strength and intensity. Long after the animal life of man has reached its highest point, and is fairly on the decline, the spirit feels itself sensibly growing; growing in the range of its intellectual grasp, growing in its power of will, growing in its sense of being a centre of life, unlike any of the forms of animal or vegetable life around it. Is it possible that death will abruptly put an end to this hitherto uninterrupted development? Is it possible that we thus continuously expand in all that constitutes our real human selves, only to find at the gate of death that we were nothing but brutes after all, although endowed with sensibilities and imaginations just keen enough to make us the victims of an immense and exceptional delusion?

It is often remarked that the Bible nowhere deals with the natural immortality of the human soul as a thesis to be proved.[1] As in the case of the soul's spirituality, the Bible scarcely asserts, but it everywhere takes the truth

[1] It is not meant that the soul of man is immortal through any internal necessity, such as might be held to belong to an uncompounded essence. In this sense God is ὁ μόνος ἔχων ἀθανασίαν (1 Tim. vi. 16). In all creatures, indestructibility is a gift. It is a gift to the spirit, as distinct from the animal life-power of man. The ancients, Tatian and Justin Martyr, who protested against the Greek idea of a necessary immortality inherent in the soul, did not deny the gift of immortality, which as a matter of fact the Creator had bestowed. Just as man conceives of God, so he conceives of eternity, and longs for it. His longing shows that he is designed from eternity; it is otherwise inexplicable. "God has placed eternity, עוֹלָם in the heart of man" (Eccles. iii. 21). It is a matter of experience; and the argumentum ab appetitu æternitatis to the reality of an eternal future is an adaptation of the Cartesian inference from the idea to the being of a God. Cf. Delitzsch, Bibl. Psych. vi. § 2.

for granted. When patriarchs and kings are said in the language of the Old Testament to be gathered to their fathers, it is not merely meant that their bones were laid in the common family resting-place. The natural scenery of Palestine probably suggested the word which described the revealed invisible home of the spirits of the dead.[1] It was "a land of darkness, as darkness itself;"[2] the common receptacle of the "small and great," of the "servant and his master," of kings and counsellors of the earth, of prisoners and of oppressors.[3] All were gathered there, under new conditions of life, incompatible with those earthly forms of activity[4] which cease at death. Not that the dead are passive or unconscious. Isaiah's description of the movement of spirits in the unseen world at the descent of the spirit of the King of Babylon can hardly be resolved into poetical license; and it is observable that the heathen monarch is there together with the rulers of Israel.[5] This doctrine of *Scheol* is perfectly consistent with the general truth that at death the human spirit returns to God,[6] and that the souls of the righteous are in "His hands," in the sense of being exempted from torment.[7] Nor is it in any way at issue with the doctrine of a bodily resurrection, which, while its early and distinct appearance in the Psalter[8] is utterly inconsistent with the theory of

[1] שְׁאוֹל is properly what is sunk deep, bent in; hence a ravine, abyss, depth. Cf. Fuerst, Lex. in voc.

[2] Job x. 21. [3] Job iii. 13-19. [4] Eccles. 9, 10. [5] Is. xiv. 9, *sqq.*

[6] Eccles. xii. 7. [7] Wisd. iii. 1.

[8] Ps. xvi. 10, 11; Acts ii. 25-31. Cf. also Ps. xlix. 16; lxxiii. 23, *sqq.*

its being due to Eastern influences[1] upon the Jewish Revelation at the period of the Captivity, does undoubtedly, in the later books, come very prominently into view. Apart from a popular belief in this doctrine, the imagery of Isaiah[2] and Ezekiel[3] would have been unintelligible to their contemporaries; and both in the dark days of the Captivity in Babylon,[4] and in the later struggle of the Maccabees against Antiochus Epiphanes, this faith in a Resurrection sustained the oppressed against the persecutors, even the martyrs in their agony.[5] So far as Alexandria influenced Judaism, it discouraged faith in a corporeal Resurrection. Philo, like a genuine Platonist, sees in death the emancipation of the soul from its bodily prison-house. But the ruling religious minds in Palestine at the time of Christ's appearance believed in the resurrection of our actual bodies.[6] Such a doctrine of course implies the immortality of the soul; but the only demonstration of the truth of the soul's immortality is given in our Lord's reply to the Sadducees on the subject of the Resurrection. He argues from the title, "the God of Abraham, the God of Isaac, and the God of Jacob," which God was pleased to claim in centuries long after the death of the patriarchs, that the patriarchs must still be living, because God is the God, not of the dead, but of the living.[7] By this general statement our

[1] As suggested by Jul. Müller, Studd. und Kritt, 1835.

[2] Is. xxvi. 14-19. [3] Ezek. xxxvii. 1-14. Cf. Hos. vi. 2; xiii. 14.

[4] Dan. xii. 1-3, 13. [5] 2 Macc. vii. 9, 11, 14, 23; xii. 42-45; xiv. 16.

[6] S. Matt. xxii. 24, *sqq.*; Acts xxiii. 8, xxiv. 15. Joseph. Ant. xviii. 1-3. Bell, Jud. ii. 8-14. Qu. by Grimm.

[7] S. Matt. xxii. 32; S. Mark xii. 27; S. Luke xx. 38.

Lord apparently implies that God does not create spiritual beings only that they may sink back into nothing. The distinctive teaching of the New Testament about the future world everywhere presupposes the soul's immortality. If death were annihilation for all of us, or for all but the just, the descriptions of the end of the world, of the last judgment,[1] of the general resurrection,[2] and of the future state,[3] would have no interest for any but a minority of mankind. It is the steady conviction that, in some way, we shall each and all personally subsist after death, which secures to these pages of our Bibles such universal interest.

This conviction of our immortality rests on what is for Christians an unquestioned certainty. In Christian eyes, the central fact of the world's annals is the Resurrection of our Lord Jesus Christ from the dead. It occurred in the full daylight of history: it was attested by hundreds of witnesses.[4] We can only deny its truth upon *à priori* principles, which are not merely destructive of serious belief that God is a Moral and even a Living Being, but which are also fatal to confidence in human history. The Resurrection of Christ is the guarantee of our own. The clouds which hung around the gate of death in earlier ages have rolled away

[1] S. Matt. xxv. 31-46; Acts xvii. 31; Rom. xiv. 10; 2 Cor. v. 10; 2 Tim. iv. 1; 1 S. Pet. iv. 5.

[2] S. John v. 28, *sqq.*; Acts xxiv. 15.

[3] Rom. ii. 10, viii. 18; 1 Cor. xiii. 12; 1 S. John iii. 2; Heb. x. 26, 27; Rev. xiv. 13; S. Matt. viii. 12; S. Mark ix. 43, *sqq.*; S. John xii. 26, xiv. 2, *sqq.*; xvii. 24; Rev. xxi. 7, 8.

[4] 1 Cor. xv. 6, *ὤφθη ἐπάνω πεντακοσίοις ἀδελφοῖς ἐφάπαξ, ἐξ ὧν οἱ πλείους μένουσιν ἕως ἄρτι, τινὲς δὲ καὶ ἐκοιμήθησαν.*

since the day of our Saviour's triumph over death; the presumptive speculations which were previously rife as to the future state have been exchanged for strong certainties. "Life and immortality have been brought to light by the Gospel:" "God has begotten us again to a lively hope, by the resurrection of Jesus Christ from the dead:" Christians are "not to sorrow as those that have no hope:" Death has lost its sting, and the grave its victory.[1]

Here, too, let it be noted, that although the soul is the seat of man's personal life, it is not, as has been already hinted, man in his completeness. Man is a body as well as a soul. Materialism itself has here done valuable service in correcting the exaggerations of a one-sided spiritualism. It is common, but erroneous, to speak of man's body as being related to his spirit only as is the casket to the jewel which it contains, or only as a prisoner to the walls of his dungeon.[2] But as a matter of fact, the personal spirit of man strikes its roots far and deep into the encompassing frame of sense, with which, from the first moment of its existence, it has been so intimately associated: in a thousand ways, and most powerfully, the body acts on the soul, and the soul on the body. They are only parted at

[1] 2 Tim. i. 10; 1 S. Pet. i. 3; 1 Thess. iv. 13; 1 Cor. xv. 55.

[2] The false spiritualism which is implied in these metaphors is, in modern times at least, chiefly due to the Cartesian philosophy. Descartes held that the human soul was made only for the purposes of *thought* (Disc. sur la Méth. pt. 5.); the animal-life of man was, as a consequence, in his judgment, merely that of an independent machine. Madame de Sévigné rallies this once popular theory "des machines qui aiment, des machines qui ont une élection pour quelqu'un, des machines qui sont jalouses, des machines qui craignent." Œuvr. t. iii. lett. 170.

death by a violent wrench. The spirit can indeed exist independently of the body, but this independent existence is not its emancipation from a prison-house of matter and sense; it is a temporary and abnormal divorce from the companion whose presence is needed to complete its life. Would the soul, permanently severed from the body, still be, properly speaking, man? Would it not really be some other being? Our inmost consciousness here echoes the answer of science. The body which has been so long the associate and partner of the soul's life, the instrument of its will, the minister of its passions, mingling lower physical sensations with that higher life of thought and feeling which belongs to it, could not be altogether cast away without impairing the completeness of our being, without imperilling the continuous identity of our changeful existence.

This, then, is the true ground of the general resurrection, which is no eccentric or gratuitous miracle, but the restoration to man of that completeness of identity which is impaired by death. If the body did not rise, man would, by dying, not simply enter upon a new stage of being; he would exist as a different order or species of creature. His moral history would have changed its conditions and character. The disembodied spirit might repudiate the weaknesses or excesses of the companion with which it had finally parted company. As a matter of fact, all men are to rise again with their bodies, and to give account of their own works: the complex being which acted here, is to be judged hereafter.

The body and soul together share here in one composite existence; each acts upon the other as well as with it. The corruptible body presseth down the soul. The passions which have their seat in the soul depict themselves upon the surface of the body. On the one hand, an Apostle reminds us that fleshly lusts war not merely against the bodily health, but against the soul.[1] On the other hand, a beautiful soul illuminates the face of a S. Stephen with angelic light;[2] and hereafter the bodies of the blessed will be "glorious," that is to say, translucent with the splendours of the glorified spirit.[3]

IV.

Religion, in order to meet the wants of human nature, will take account of man's composite being: she will have lower relations to the bodies as well as higher relations to the souls of men. As man has, besides his unseen person, an outward and visible shape, so will religion herself provide sensible forms as well as supersensuous realities. She will exact outward as well as inward reverence, because in a composite being like man, the one is really the condition of the other. There are bodily postures which absolutely forbid heavenly exercises to the soul: to lounge in an arm-chair is inconsistent with the tension of thought

[1] 1 S. Pet. ii. 11. [2] Acts vi. 15. [3] 1 Cor. xv. 43.

and will which belongs to adoration of the Most Holy. Religion, like man himself, is a beautiful spirit tabernacling in a body of sense; her divine and immutable truths are shrouded beneath the unrivalled poetry of Bible language; her treasures of grace beneath the outward and visible signs which meet us in sacraments. She proclaims the invisible by that which meets the eye; she heralds the eternal harmonies by a music that falls upon the ear. She certainly is not all form, for man is not a brute; but also she is not all spirit, for man is not an angel. She deals with man as being precisely what he is, and she enlists the lower faculties of his being in aid of the higher. Yet if she is true to man and to herself, she never allows him to forget the unseen in the seen, the inward in the outward, the soul in the body. For religious purposes, the soul must always be incomparably of the highest importance, as being the very man himself, the man in the secret recesses of his being, the man at the imperishable centre of his life, the man as he lives beneath the Eye, and enters into relations with the Heart of his infinite Creator.

Certainly if belief in our being personal spirits is essential to religion, and belief in the immediate creation of the soul by God is stimulating to it, belief in the soul's immortality is of yet higher religious importance. The relation between God and the soul, in which religion consists, would be little more to us than a sentiment or a literary taste, if we were persuaded that we should have taken leave of it, as we shall have taken leave of our clothes and of our books, when we are laid in our coffins. Would religion be worth our attention as serious men, would it be anything more than a plaything, if all really ended at death? That the soul is immortal, standing in its immortality, for weal or woe, face to face with the Everlasting God;—this truth, dimly grasped by natural religion, has been wrought into the very heart and fibre of Christendom. It is taken for granted by Christian faith just as naturally as is the fact of life itself. It underlies that sense of an eternal life which good men already enjoy here, and which implies not simply a consciousness that admits of no idea of succession or time, but an immortal soul in fixed communion with an Eternal Object. It teaches man to look upon all the acts and habits which really feed and strengthen religion as a part of his preparation and outfit for eternity, to be in some sense carried with him as he crosses the heights which form his present horizon, and which shut out from his view the eternal world. And thus it has elevated and enriched human nature in a thousand ways, which we only do not sufficiently appreciate because we are so entirely accustomed to them.

Let me illustrate this by an example. Putting religion for the moment out of the question altogether, there is no doubt as to the view which a philanthropist must take of suicide, supposing it to become general, and regarding it in its influence upon society. When a popular Cyrenaic teacher, Hegesias, advocated suicide, at Alexandria, as being the course upon which a really wise man would resolve after comparing the sum of the pleasures of life with the sum of its misfortunes, Ptolemy felt it necessary, in the interests of good government and of society, to oblige him to close his lecture-room. But the sentiment with which suicide is practically regarded among us is not based on any mere estimate of its social bearings, still less is it looked upon only as a mode of passing out of life. The announcement that this or that well-known man had destroyed himself would create in any modern society a sensation distinct in kind from that which would be caused by the simple announcement of his death.[1] Why is this? It is because Christianity, revealing to man as a certainty the fact of his immortality, has given a new meaning, value, solemnity to life. To live is to be on our trial, with a tremendous future immediately before us; and to shorten this trial by a voluntary act, is, apart from other and even graver aspects of such an act, felt to be altogether irreconcileable with this, the Christian estimate of life.[2]

Considering the strength of the instinct of self-preservation which is naturally implanted in us, suicide shocks us as being a violent contradiction of that instinct. Yet while cases of suicide are to be found here and there, in all times and districts of history, there have been periods and places when suicide has been nothing less than a passion

[1] Since this observation was made, it has been painfully illustrated in the case of the lamented M. Prêvost-Paradol.

[2] Lecky, "History of European Morals," ii. 52. "Direct and deliberate suicide, which occupies so prominent a place in the moral history of antiquity, almost absolutely disappeared within the Church." Cf. pp. 40–63 of this interesting chapter.

—a moral epidemic swaying the imaginations and wills of whole classes even of educated men. In India suicide has been for at least two thousand years the result of energetic conviction; it is still what it was at the date of Alexander's conquest. It is at this day the effort by which the individual would plunge into the infinite, in which it is his presumed happiness to forfeit his individuality; whether that infinite be the supreme soul of the Brahmins, or the Nirvâna of the Buddhists. In Greece and Rome, suicide was a precept not of religion but of philosophy. It was recommended by philosophies the most opposed to each other. In Greece the great representatives of the Cynic school, Zeno, Diogenes, and in Christian times, Peregrinus, died by their own hands. The Cyrenaics formulated the doctrine of suicide, as an escape from the preponderating miseries of life. At Rome, Lucretius, the Epicurean poet, as well as Cato and Brutus, under Stoic influences, destroyed themselves. The Epicurean feeling, that when life had been made the most of for the purposes of enjoyment it was time to end it, coincided as to its practical result with the Stoic doctrine that the stern effort by which man could in extremity make good his self-mastery is a voluntary death. Of this doctrine Seneca is the great master. Suicide is, he contends, the act by which man asserts his rights over himself, when face to face with the menaces and oppressions of tyranny: suicide is the door though which liberty may retire from a world of slaves.

This doctrine especially it was which dictated suicide

on a considerable scale in the first of the three periods when like a moral plague it has darkened the life of Europe. During the later days of the Roman Republic, and under the stern Cæsarism of the Empire, suicide was recommended and practised as an escape from the political and social evils of the time. The spirit of suicide only fell back before the advance of the Church; and more than three centuries after Seneca, we find S. Augustine combating his arguments one by one in the closing books of the treatise on the City of God. The second period was that of the Renaissance in the sixteenth century. Suicide had nearly disappeared during the Middle Ages; but when educated Italy, with Leo X. at its head, had saturated itself afresh with Paganism, it was natural that some of the moral ideas of antiquity should reappear in the train of so engrossing a study of its mind and style. Philippo Strozzi, the prisoner of the Grand Duke Cosmo I., destroys himself, praying God—it is an odd mixture of Christian and Pagan creeds—that his soul may be placed along with the soul of Cato of Utica, and of others who have died after the same fashion. Montaigne in his essays defends suicide elaborately; and in time it had its devotees in England, no less than in France and Italy. The more positive and earnest Christianity of the seventeenth century brought with it a more worthy appreciation of the real seriousness of life: but in the succeeding age the taste for suicide was renewed, not as a part of the complete Pagan ideal of conduct, but as the fruit of a melancholy estimate of our condition in this world, joined to impaired or decomposing religious convictions. The felt disappointments of life as a whole, the absence of fixed aims, the culture of imagination and passion without any regulating faith, the feverish indecision, the languid yet ever-growing self-idolatry, the moral atmosphere of impatience, irritation, curiosity, the mingled rapture and pain of vagrant imagination, the utter caprice and prostration of will,—these were the characteristics of a period which was impersonated by, and which recognized itself at length in Goethe. In the earnestness as well as in the levity of an irreligious age, the ordinary motives to self-destruction acquired a new and fatal force; and the growing evil was only checked by the Christian reaction which followed on the French Revolution throughout Europe; and which again restored belief in the solemnity of life by forcing men to look steadily at the eternity which succeeds it. Certainly, we have only to refer to yesterday's paper [1] to read the account of a suicide from London Bridge. Domestic misfortunes, temporary derangement, moral despair, still count their too numerous tale of victims. But it is a simple matter of fact that belief in a future state, as taught by Christ and His Apostles, is the one adequate antidote to this weird contempt for the gift of existence—a contempt which cannot really extinguish the gift which it yet can so irretrievably curse.[2]

[1] *Standard*, March 19, 1870.

[2] On this subject the opening Essay in M. Caro's Nouvelles Etudes Morales is full of interest; and I am indebted to it in the foregoing paragraphs.

It would be easy to shew in like manner how—sometimes directly, sometimes indirectly—Christianity has bettered the condition of the masses of mankind by making Christians feel the value of each separate life. Our Lord has done this, as no other has done it: nowhere is human life thought so highly of as where the Christian creed is sincerely believed to be absolute truth. The history of infanticide is one among other illustrations of this result of a hearty belief in immortality. The great Christian doctrines centre in, they are unintelligible apart from, faith in the value of the individual soul. The soul's value is measured in a Christian's judgment by the stupendous truth of the Incarnation and Death of the Everlasting Son; by the gift and energies of the Divine Spirit; by the perpetual intercession of Christ in heaven; by the grace and power of the Sacraments; by the prospects which open to faith's eye beyond the grave—upwards into an illimitable heaven, downwards into a fathomless hell. Confronted with each of these truths, the soul confidently, yet tremblingly, feels its dignity—its priceless dignity—in the eye of its Maker. The soul feels as if, when it turns awhile from the daily round of duty to gather itself up into itself, to sink a shaft into the depths of its consciousness, there were two, and only two, beings in existence—itself and its God. To know more of Him, to love Him more, to serve Him better—this is its constant effort; and its hope and prayer is to receive day by day, in larger measures, more abundant communications of His mind and of His life. In a word, when dwelling on the soul's nature and destiny, man understands that religion is his highest and most reasonable field of thought and work.

It has indeed been said that the old phrase of "saving one's soul" has ceased to have much meaning for the religion of educated people in the present day. If this be indeed true, we can only rejoin, in all truth and sorrow, "so much the worse for the educated people." Whatever be a man's place in society or in letters, whatever his circumstances in this earthly scene, it remains true that, to close with the offers which Christ makes to sinners, to "work out his salvation with fear and trembling," is his one most important business here. The eternal realities do not change with our intellectual fashions; and like the laws which govern our physical frames, the spiritual rules under which men live or die are the same for all of us. The day will come when the God-fearing peasants of Devonshire or of Yorkshire will rise in judgment against the cultured irreligion of the centres of our modern civilisation: not because it is cultured, but because it is irreligion; because in the glare of its enthusiasms for the additions which it has made to the knowledge of our material home and structure, it has forgotten almost or altogether the Eternal Home beyond.

The salvation of the soul can only be treated as an old-world anachronism, when it is clear either that man has no real soul, or that it does not survive death, or that if it does survive, its condition hereafter has no reference whatever to its state and actions here. If this be really meant, it is better to say so; only, in that case, it is difficult to see what sphere is left for religion at all. If it be not meant, then, undoubtedly, a variety of the gravest questions at once open before us, both as to what we have to be saved from, and as to the means and conditions of our salvation. Upon the first of these questions, we shall encounter in the next lecture some of the more serious differences which divide the modern world: to-day it must suffice to have insisted upon the mingled blessedness and awfulness of life. What it is to live here at all as a human being; what it is to possess or rather to be a centre of self-reflecting thought, of self-determining will, a centre of life which under some conditions will be perpetuated indefinitely;—this, when we think of it steadily and in good earnest, is, next to the spiritual sight of God Himself, the most solemn, the most chastening, the most stimulating consideration that can open upon us. Let us make much of it, in the interests both of the present and of the future, for the sake of God and truth, as well as of our own lasting happiness. Let us determine to ask ourselves again and again during the coming week, what in our inmost selves we really are, and, next, whither we are going. Let us listen to a voice which will at times find some echo in every conscience, and which bids us, in God's name, reflect that "the things which are seen are temporal, while the things which are not seen are eternal."

LECTURE IV.

Fourth Sunday in Lent.

THE OBSTACLE TO RELIGION—SIN.

S. James i. 15.

When desire hath conceived, it bringeth forth sin; and sin, when it is finished, bringeth forth death.

THE ground which we have hitherto traversed is, in the main, common ground to those who accept the idea of religion in any serious sense at all. Religion is impossible, except as a bond between a real, that is to say, a moral and governing God, and a real, that is to say, a conscious, self-determining, immortal soul. Deny either term of the statement, and religion dissolves into an unpractical sentiment, which either has no adequate object, or else no adequate subject and field for its existence. Hitherto, therefore, at least generally, we have occupied positions which may be taken up even by theories which are very earnestly opposed to some of the most distinctive features of the Christian creed. But to-day we advance a step further; and this advance, it is well to say at the outset, must forfeit the sympathy of many who have thus far been able to accompany us. We have reached a point at which we encounter a fact of such widespread and deep significance, that it must perforce colour and impress any real religion, from first to last; so that its pressure and importance are felt both in the drift and substance of religious belief, and in the characteristic temper and dispositions of a religious mind. The fact in question is moral evil. Moral evil, or sin, is the disturbing and disorganizing force which breaks up the original relationship of love and confidence between God and man. In view of moral evil, revelation must be not merely illuminative, but remedial; and religion, in order to be true to the facts of human nature, must consist predominantly of penitence and contrition. And Christianity is broadly at issue with not a few of the religious proposals which aspire to take its place in the present day on this very ground. It does, and they do not, practically recognize this universal and fundamental fact: they do, and it will not, consent to gloss it over, or to explain it away, or to assume that man's religious wants can be really satisfied without looking it boldly in the face, and providing against it a cure and an antidote.

It would be a very great error to suppose that Christianity has invented the idea of sin only for the purpose of remedying it. If sin were not a fact independent of Christianity; if it were not an integral feature of human life, Christianity would long ago have perished. In the spiritual world, too, there is such a thing as supply and demand; and if a religion pre-supposes wants which do not exist, and brings remedies for diseases of which nobody is conscious, it has already signed its death-warrant. It is true that Christianity, as a revelation of the highest moral truth, has, beyond any other religion, educated man's sense of sin; but this sense of sin was not itself a result of Christianity. Long before Christ came, the moral sin and sickness of the world was felt, rather than explicitly recognized. It was of course recognized by the educated conscience of Israel, with its moral law, creating a knowledge of sin, and its sacrificial system, deepening the sense of the guilt of sin, and its prophetic ministry, bringing these general truths home with an unflinching courage and precision to the sinful kings and populations of the later centuries of its history. But this heart-sickness of the world was also a fact very vividly present to the comparatively uneducated conscience of Greece. What makes a great heathen say that even if death does involve endless unconsciousness, it ought, nevertheless, to be looked upon as substantial gain; a deep sleep throughout a lifetime, a sleep unbroken by dreams, being, in his opinion, preferable to the active life of the most fortunate of mankind? Probably he could not have told us the real reason; this was an instinct of his rather than a reasoned judgment. He instinctively perceived that in human life, as he saw it, even under its brightest aspects, there was on the whole more evil than good. More evil than good,—but not merely or chiefly more physical evil. The natural courage of a great soul would never have regarded a preponderance of misfortune or of pain in a human life as a reason for wishing to be practically non-existent. The evil which decided the balance of judgment against the expediency of life, was more penetrating, more oppressive, more fatal to the sense of having a right to live than any pain of body, or loss of friends or of goods could possibly be. It was, in a word, moral evil. The heathen knew of the existence of moral evil, but they had very imperfect ideas of its extent and nature. They knew that there was a right and a wrong, to which man is bound to conform himself; but what is right and what is wrong, and why right is right, and wrong is wrong, these were subjects upon which their knowledge was exceeding imperfect. But the general fact of man's disloyalty to such moral truth, as he knew, is often admitted by the leading minds of antiquity. They acknowledge man's secret misery; his proneness to yield to temptations which his conscience condemns; his forfeiture of the light which he actually enjoys by disobedience to its requirements. "I see and approve of the better course," says Horace, "I follow the worse." "Nature has given us small sparks of knowledge," says Cicero, "we corrupt and extinguish them by our immoralities." "We are all wicked," says Seneca, "what one of us blames in another, each will find in his own bosom."[1]

The Epistle to the Romans itself, which sets out by shewing that both the Jewish and Gentile worlds, by

[1] Quoted by Luthardt.

reason of the sin which had overmastered them, stood in need of the justifying righteousness of Christ, is scarcely more explicit in its assertions than are these great heathen. For to observe human life at all, and to reflect on the observation, is to be conscious of its moral anomalies. This consciousness often takes the disguised form of a bitter complaint against the external conditions, nay, the very fact of life itself. So it was at the end of the last century. Werther translated Hamlet into the language of modern life, and Goethe made Werther European. Werther embodied the philosophy of melancholy; of dissatisfaction with life, grounded on a sense of hopeless irretrievable failure. In days nearer to our own, this Pessimism has found a prophet in Schopenhauer, the philosopher of Frankfort. "The history of every life," he says, "is but a history of suffering; the course of life is generally but a series of greater or of less misfortunes. The true sense of the monologue in Hamlet may be thus summed up. Our condition is so wretched that utter annihilation would be decidedly preferable." . . . "The oft-lamented shortness of life may perhaps be its best attribute." . . . "Life," he pursues, "may be represented as a constant deceiver in things both great and small. If it makes promises, it never keeps them, except to shew how undesirable is that which was desired. First the hope, then the thing hoped for, disappoints us. Life gives only to take away. The charm of distance shews us a paradise, which vanishes like an optical delusion, if we allow ourselves to approach it. Hence our happiness ever lies in the future or in the past; the present may be compared to a dark cloud which the wind drives before it over the sunny plain; behind it there is the sunshine, beneath it a constant shadow. Life is consequently ever unsatisfying; the future being uncertain, the past irrecoverable. Life with its hourly, daily, weekly, and yearly, little, great, and greater discomforts; with its disappointments, its misfortunes, baffling all calculation; bears so plainly the impress of something which is to be spoilt to us, that it is difficult to imagine how this could ever have been mistaken, and how any one could have conceived that life was given to be thankfully enjoyed, or man made to be happy. The general structure of life would rather produce the conviction that nothing is worth our efforts, our energies, and our struggles; that all possessions are vanity, the world a bankrupt in all quarters, and life a business which does not pay its expenses. Satisfaction and prosperity are merely negative—merely the absence of suffering; only sorrow and want can be positively felt." . . . "We do not perceive that certain days of our lives have been happy till they have given place to unhappy ones. If, then, there were a hundred times less sorrow in the world than there is, its mere existence would be enough to confirm a truth expressed in various ways, though always with some indirectness—namely, that the existence of the world is a matter not of rejoicing but of grief; that its annihilation would be preferable to its existence; that it is fundamentally something which ought not to exist. Human life, far from wearing the aspect of a gift, has every appearance of an incurred debt, the payment of which is exacted in the form of the urgent necessities, the tormenting desires, the unceasing want which life involves. The whole period of life is generally consumed in the liquidation of this debt, and yet it is only the interest which can be thus paid off. The payment of the capital is effected by death."[1]

Such is Schopenhauer's reply to the sunny Optimism of Leibnitz, who deems this "the best of possible worlds"; and in this philosophy of despair we listen to the same chord as that already struck by the Platonic Socrates, only the despair is deeper and sadder than was possible for a heathen, who had never heard of a Christian's hope. For Schopenhauer might also seem at times to be expanding and paraphrasing S. Paul's picture of the whole creation groaning and travailing in pain together until now; only S. Paul saw light upon the distant horizon, and he knew the secret of the present distress. It was moral evil which had introduced this unrest and disorder, or which, if it had not introduced all physical suffering into the universe, at least had made it so intolerable. The aggravated, unappeasable restlessness which results from a conscious forfeiture of the harmony of our being with the moral law of the universe;—this it is which quickens the agony of that piteous wail to which we have just been listening:

[1] Schopenhauer, Die Welt als Wille und Vorstellung, § 67, 59, ii. 46, qu. by Luthardt, Apolog. Vortr. Vorles, 2, Notes.

this it is which lights up in the human consciousness the sense of an almost infinite capacity for pain.

I.

The presence and power of moral evil in the world has ever afforded matter for the persevering, anxious, weary exercise of human thought. The difficulties of the problem have not silenced inquiry; the failure of one generation of thinkers has not discouraged another. Like the movements of the heavenly bodies, or the laws of health, the existence of moral evil is too patent, too importunate a subject, to be permanently set aside by human beings: it exerts over all who seriously consider the meaning and facts of life too irresistible a fascination not to demand from each generation some attempt at accounting for it, however others may have failed to do so. And in dealing with this problem let us observe that there are two fatal tendencies, which beset, on this side and on that, the necessary path of inquiry with the importunity of a resistless fascination. Like Scylla and Charybdis, they divide between them the great majority of those who would attempt a passage; to escape from the one is generally to fall a victim to the attractions or violence of the other. Our path then lies between the temptation to extenuate the idea of evil, and the temptation to tamper with the idea of God.

1. Of these, the more welcome to the spirit of our time is the former. It is impossible to deny that moral evil exists; but is it impossible to soften that stern idea of evil which haunts the human conscience, and which is sanctioned by Revelation? May not moral evil be represented as a necessary product of man's nature and constitution, as the mere expression and symptom of his place among created beings, nay, even as an indispensable condition of his turning his opportunities to the best account and of fulfilling his destiny? Yes, it has been said, sin in man is only the measure of his failure to achieve ideal or metaphysical perfection. Man is confessedly a finite being; and the evil which clings to him, or which he does, is but an appropriate feature of his original circumstances. "The good is that which is, or the real: evil begins with that which is not, or with the unreal." Therefore the Unbounded, All-powerful Being is alone the good, because of His Infinity and Almightiness. Creatures are partly good and partly evil; they are good so far as they exist; their evil begins with their finitude; it begins at the point where their little life shades oft through weakness into non-existence. In this sense too, "whatever is, is right:" whatever tries to be, and cannot be, is wrong. Sin and weakness, strength and virtue, are interchangeable terms. Man as a moral agent suffers in two ways for this metaphysical imperfection of his life. His knowledge of duty is very limited, so that, while he really aims at what is good he constantly does something less than good, only

from want of that enlarged information which is denied him by the limited conditions of his being. And he is also tied down to a gross material body, filled with sensual impulses and instincts, which control and overmaster his loftier aspirations. His sensuous nature necessarily and perpetually depresses the level of his thought and action; and in this depression, thus physically necessitated, from the line of his ideal attainments to that of his actual attainments, consists his sin.

Now, so far is sin from being the product of imperfect knowledge, that the imperfection of man's knowledge is the measure of his innocence. Knowledge is essential to responsibility; the latter can only exist in the ratio of the former. The lower creatures cannot sin against the knowledge which we have, but which they do not possess: we cannot sin against a higher knowledge than that which has been vouchsafed to us. But we know enough to have enormous opportunities for sin open to us; and when we do sin, our consciences do not whisper that had we known more we might have been innocent still. Omniscience is not a condition of virtue; philosophers are not always saints, nor little children always criminals. Nor is sin accurately attributed to the necessary action of our sensuous nature. It is not, by any means, universally or even generally the product of insurgent senses. Ruinous as are the sins for which perverted sensual instincts furnish the material, there are many sins of the darkest type which have nothing to do with sense. We should be just as capable of envy and hatred, of ambition and pride, of untruthfulness, or the desire to destroy a fellow-creature, if we had no bodies at all. Sin then, as such, is not the irrepressible product of a sensuous body; nor is it the imperfection of moral or spiritual effort which alliance to such a body is thought of necessity to imply. In order to practise virtue, it is indeed often necessary, with the Apostle, to keep under our body and bring it into subjection;[1] but the body does not exert any irresistible power of depression over the higher instincts of the soul, or it would be useless to struggle against it. The seat of sin is in the will, whether sin be chiefly spiritual or sensual; the body merely furnishes one of the spheres wherein temptation may be found and sin is possible; and sin is a much graver thing than any failure to attain ideal goodness which arises from our being weighted with a body of sense. If sin were only inevitable weakness; if it were nothing more serious than a lowly condition in the scale of being resulting from man's physical circumstances; the conscience of man would no more torture him on account of it than the conscience of the cripple or the blind accuses him of his misfortune. Sin differs from virtue not as a flower which has been frostbitten differs from a flower which has escaped the frost, but as a self-made devil differs from an angel; and the body can no more fetter the will of the saint than the triumph of its rebellious senses can be held to measure or diminish the responsibility of the sinner.

[1] 1 Cor. ix. 27.

So faint an estimate of evil may help us to create a morality that shall accommodate itself to human life as it actually is. It will not furnish us for long with a standard of moral truth which will remind us of what our life actually is not. It may recommend itself at once, and very persuasively, to our self-love. It were pleasant to think, if we could think, that we have never been in the terrible predicament of opposing and refusing a known standard of goodness; that, at the worst, we are only pardonable and even interesting instances of failure to be all that we conceivably might have been. To see in evil nothing beyond the result of man's finite nature; to see in it a privation only and not a contradiction of good, is undoubtedly calculated to put us all on very good terms with ourselves. But is any theory of the kind consistent with the most rudimentary idea of evil? Surely our consciences tell us that evil is a great deal more than a maimed effort at goodness, more than a privation of goodness which might be but is not. Evil and good are not, so to put it, upon the same line of advance, with only this difference, that while goodness is success, evil is failure. If, for instance, I tell a very deliberate lie, with a view to getting possession of a sum of money by doing so, I surely do something more than fail to reach an ideal of perfect truthfulness. I move very deliberately in an opposite direction to that of truth; I do not come short of it; I contradict and trample it under foot. If nobody ever told a lie without wishing to tell the truth, while yet he failed, from defective knowledge, to do so perfectly, this theory of evil as the symptom of man's finite nature might at least claim a hearing. As it is, the real facts of every human conscience are against it.

And accordingly Holy Scripture speaks of sin in terms which are utterly at variance with any such estimate of moral evil as this. It speaks of "sin having dominion over us,"[1] and of the justified being "dead unto sin;"[2] but we are not ruled by imperfect forms of goodness, nor do we "die" to moral efforts which were only less successful than our present ones. It speaks of sin as a service, the wages of which is death;[3] as a defilement from which we must be cleansed and washed;[4] as a bondage from which Christ makes us free.[5] There is, it appears, a law of sin in our members, to which we may be brought into captivity;[6] and sin it is which constitutes the sting of death,[7] and which in its deliberate and emphatic form is the death of the soul.[8] How is all this language, which presupposes an energetic contradiction to exist between sin and holiness, to be reconciled with any representation of sin as being merely imperfection, whether of knowledge or of moral force? As if there were no sins except those of negligence and omission, no sins of set purpose to do evil; as if there were no such thing as knowing evil to be evil, and deliberately embracing it![9]

[1] Rom. vi. 14. [2] Rom. vi. 2. [3] Rom. vi. 23; cf. 1 S. John iii. 8.
[4] Ps. li. 2-7; Isa. i. 16; Jerem. iv. 14; Acts xxii. 16; 1 Cor. vi. 11; Rev. i. 5; Rev. vii. 14.
[5] Rom. vi. 16-22. [6] Rom. vii. 23. [7] 1 Cor. xv. 56.
[8] 1 S. John v. 16. [9] Rom. i. 32.

Indeed, to represent sin as something due to the original imperfection of human nature is to contradict the sanctity and justice of God. God is the Maker of His creatures; and if creatures are imperfect, as compared with the Creator, it is from the necessity of the case, because the creature is not the Creator. But this inherent or metaphysical imperfection does not necessarily imply moral imperfection: had it been so, God could not have created at all without violating His own attributes. And certainly, if man only sins because his views of absolute good are limited, and his higher aspirations weighed down by the body of sense which encompasses him, the author of that intellectual finiteness and of that sensual frame is the author of man's sin; and God, in creating, forfeits His sanctity, and in forfeiting His sanctity ceases to be the object of religion.

This conclusion, indeed, is not declined by the Pantheistic philosophy, and by that large body of thought in our day, which is profoundly, because for the most part unconsciously, moulded by it. Sin, we are told, like everything else, is really due to the Divine activity; but, then, sin is not without its uses—I had almost said, its merits. It is, forsooth, the stimulant and condition of goodness. As in the world of Hegelian thought, truth, we are told, is not to be looked for in any single and direct affirmations, but only as the term of a series of contradictions, which not only may be true together, but are together necessary to express the full truth; so it has been asserted, that in the moral sphere there is a somewhat similar law of contradictories; that it is as unphilosophical to find fault with what is vulgarly described as sin, as it is to keep no terms with what is coarsely described as falsehood. Sin is the necessary foil to goodness: without sin goodness would never be roused into active life. Contradiction is a condition of moral life: goodness is not tranquil conformity to law, but energetic struggle against that which contradicts it, and which by contradicting it makes it what it is. "Just as nature is made up of contrasts, and in it we see light opposed to darkness, and heat to cold, and expansion to concentration, and pleasure to pain, and health to sickness,—even so does the true life of the human soul emerge from deep contrasts; it is only developed by the encounter between truth and falsehood, between good and evil." . . . "Evil is thus a condition, almost an ingredient of good. Goodness would slumber in itself, it would be without the necessary impulse to exertion, unless it were constantly kept on the alert by the antagonistic energies and excesses of evil."[1]

This singular travestie of the account which the revelation has given of the permission of moral evil in the world, involves a fallacy of confusion. It confounds the good ends which evil, against its nature, may subserve in the purposes of an overruling Providence, with the inherent qualities of evil itself. Certainly it is better for the health of the body that latent disease should shew itself in pronounced illness; and when such illness is over, a patient may be all the stronger and better for having

[1] Cf. quot. by Klotz, in his art. Sünde.

been ill. But for all that, disease is disease, and not a variegated form of health; and a man in whom disease had never been latent, and whose constitution had been even monotonously free from its assaults, will be, at least, as well as another who may have happily survived a scarlet fever. What God in His loving Omnipotence may make evil do in spite of its nature is one thing; what it is in itself is another. Vice is not a necessary aliment, it is not even a necessary foil to virtue. The devil is not necessary to the existence of God; and goodness does not depend either for its beauty or its strength upon the antagonistic efforts of sin. If it were so, we should at once reach the practical conclusion of the Materialistic philosophy, which denies the existence of any free will in man whatever, and sees in all moral actions, whatever their colouring, the inevitable result of antecedents which create them, by as necessary a law as any which rules the world of matter. Upon Materialistic principles, the murderer Traupmann ought never to have been executed: he was no more responsible for his atrocities than a flash of lightning or a wave would be for the destruction of a human life. But upon the principles of the æsthetic Pantheism, it might even have been questioned whether French society did not on the whole gain by his horrible activity: and whether one who had done so much to exhibit the virtue of respect for human life in high relief, by so emphatically contradicting it, was not, in consideration of his services, entitled to receive some higher and more substantial reward than a reprieve of the penalty which he actually suffered.

Indeed, it is here that we see how irreconcileable any such theory is with the plainest instincts of a healthy conscience. If evil is necessary to the existence of good, why should conscience condemn evil? How can conscience condemn that which is necessary to the good which it approves? How, if we are to pursue this line of thought, can we ultimately avoid acquiescing in a theory which, denying all distinctions of right and wrong as of the nature of baseless prejudice, sees in evil, as in good, only an energetic manifestation of life apart from any moral colouring whatever? A last protest may indeed be made to the effect that man's business is to contradict the metaphysical necessity for evil by the moral demand that it should be resisted. But this very demand, if it is to be enforced, must proceed upon the serious conviction that moral evil is evil; that it is a something which need not be; and that if we will, we are individually and perfectly free to accept or to reject it.

Theories such as these are in truth expedients for representing sin as being less serious than it is; for softening the repulsive contrasts which it presents to holiness; for securing to it a right to feel at home in human conduct and in the human soul. Every such theory attempts to put forth a more or less disguised justification and apology on behalf of sin, at the bar of intellect, that sin may, if possible, be received without dishonour, if it be not welcomed at the court of conscience. But conscience, when she is not benumbed or asleep, must protest implacably against these attempts to make sin respectable. She can see in them only so many invitations addressed to the single soul, bidding it look tolerantly or fondly on the sure instrument of its degradation and ruin; so many invitations addressed to human society, bidding it recognize or welcome the foe who is sworn to impede and to destroy the indispensable conditions of its coherence and progress.

2. It has indeed been the dread of softening down the idea of evil which has led the human conscience in very early ages to tamper with the idea of God. The instinctive recoil from the one error has plunged it into the other. The physical evil of pain, of disease, of death, inflicts itself upon the senses; and conscience accounts for physical evil by tracing it to moral evil. Conscience cannot deny the malignity of moral evil without dethroning herself. But why should moral evil exist? The All-Holy could not have created it: to have done so would have been to cease to be Himself. But why did He permit it? And who gave it being, that He should permit it?

In ages and civilizations when the idea of God was imperfect or impoverished, men accounted for the existence of evil by ascribing it to a being or principle, coeval with God, independent of Him, and of course opposed to Him. Whether this evil was supposed to be matter out of which the Good God had fashioned the world, or whether it was conceived of as something more spiritual, the object and origin of the system was identical. It was an effort to account for the great perplexing mystery—the existence of evil. It is impossible, argued these ancient thinkers, that moral life and death, that good and evil, can flow from a single source. It is impossible that a Holy God can have been the author of evil. Evil, then, must be referred to some other origin: it must have had an author of its own. So far we cannot but follow; but then the argument appeals, in order to sustain its own false inference, to the gigantic proportions which evil has actually assumed. Considering how world-wide and imperial is the sway of evil, must not evil, it asks, be referred to some person, principle, force, or tendency, higher and older than created things; to some almighty source, existing side by side with the Author and Source of goodness, in eternal contradiction to His mind and work?

If we take the ancient Parsee doctrine as a sample, we find, in the lines of the Bundehesch, the good and evil principles—Ormuzd and Ahriman—contrasted as follows:—

> "Ormuzd is the light;
> This light is without beginning;
> Ormuzd is on high,
> Ormuzd is Holy,
> Ormuzd hath all knowledge."

On the other hand—

> "Ahriman is in darkness;
> This darkness is without beginning;
> Ahriman is in the depths;
> Ahriman delighteth in strife;
> Ahriman hath only a derived knowledge."[1]

Here, while Ahriman is in respect of knowledge the inferior of Ormuzd, they are represented as coeval; al-

[1] Ahardanesch, qu. by Hanneberg from Jos. Müller, art. Parsismus.

though the modern Parsees, especially when in conflict with Christianity, have tended, by exalting Ormuzd alone, to approach more and more closely to a practical Monotheism.[1] But there is no real question as to the practical Dualism of the earlier doctrine, which prevailed in Persia at least from the date of Darius Hystaspes to that of Alexander the Great, and again after the fall of the Parthian dynasty,—the doctrine which is confronted in the pages of the Hebrew Scriptures. In Isaiah, the God of Israel proclaims—

> "I am the Lord,
> And there is none else:
> There is no God beside Me. . . . . . .
> I form the light and create darkness;
> I make peace and create evil;
> I the Lord do all these things."[2]

Here we have a revelation probably designed to protect the faith of Israel against the Dualistic influences to which it would be exposed during the later period of the Captivity. The Eternal Lord of Heaven was much more ancient than this antagonism of good and evil which meets men's eyes in the world, and which suggested the faith from which was evolved the Zendavesta. The evil principle itself was in this sense only created by Him, that He had formed the wills which, in their perverted freedom, gave it birth. "I am the Lord, and there is none else."

[1] Cf. Hanneberg, who quotes Wilson, "The Parsee Religion," Bombay, 1843, p. 107. It would seem that the superiority of Ormuzd was never supposed to imply his power of preventing the birth of Ahriman or of annihilating him.

[2] Isa. xlv. 5, 6, 7.

In Christian times we find S. Paul insisting upon the truism, as it appears to us, that "every creature of God is good, and nothing to be despised,"[1] as a reason for rejecting certain distinctions of food which were insisted on by some ancient ascetics at Ephesus. But here he is really combating another form of the doctrine of Two Principles; which held matter to be the seat and source of evil, and certain kinds of food to be peculiarly representative of the grossness of matter. When Augustine, in a later age, as a still unconverted young man, giving the freest license both to sensual passions and to intellectual enterprise, was casting about for a theory which would at once countenance his excesses, and furnish him with a working philosophical explanation of the universe, he found it in Manicheeism. Manicheeism was the Dualism which had acquired a Christian flavour by coming into contact with Christianity; and we may form some idea of the strength and fascination of the theory, by observing how tenacious was its hold upon the strong and beautiful mind of the greatest of the Fathers, even when the full light of Catholic truth was already breaking upon him.

Isaiah's words will have already suggested that seriously to believe in two eternal principles is fatal to serious belief in the existence of God. God is the one Self-existent Being; the Maker of all things, visible and invisible. To assert that another—whether essence, person, or even matter—existed eternally side by side with God, is to deny

[1] 1 Tim. iv. 4.

God's first and necessary prerogative, as the Alone Eternal, and Self-existent. If God is to be screened in human thought from the blasphemy which would credit Him with the origination of evil, it must be by some doctrine which, unlike Dualism, does not virtually annihilate Him in order to do so.

But the doctrine of Two Principles does not succeed even in its main object, namely, the protection and affirmation of the unimpaired idea of evil itself. Evil is, in its quaintly perverted estimate, rather a growth of nature than the free product of a created will: evil has a positive substance of its own. Evil must therefore be conquered by a physical rather than a spiritual or moral treatment. This would seem to have been the idea of these mistaken ascetics at Colossæ,[1] whom S. Paul observed and reproved. And the error leads to consequences beyond itself. If evil is physical, there is no more reason for distress at a habit of lying, than at tuberculation of the lungs. If sin is physical, remedies may or may not succeed; and a moral struggle is on the whole less reasonable than a torpid resignation.

At any rate, it may be said, we of this generation are not Dualists: and what good is to be done by disinterring and gibbeting the corpses of ancient errors? But let us recollect that when error is buried as a formal theory, it often leaves behind it a miasma which infects the world of thought for many a succeeding generation. We practi-

[1] Col. ii. 22, 23.

cally affirm a second evil principle in the universe when we acquiesce in the notion that evil in ourselves or in others, in individuals or in societies, is invincible. We do not talk of a second principle; we assume one. We assume not merely a powerful but an unconquerable devil, when we despair of expelling, by God's grace, that which is evil in ourselves or in others. We bow, as we say, to the inevitable; we recognize such and such tendencies of the times. They are perhaps at issue with what we know to be right. But there they are; the current flows all one way and with increasing strength, and we say that it is useless to attempt to make head against it. Instead of overcoming evil with good, like the Apostle, we philosophically resign ourselves to being overcome with evil. But our notion of the invincibility of sin and error is at issue with our still professed faith in the one All-Powerful and Holy God. Our faint-heartedness, our despair, our abject fatalism in presence of evil, within and around us, is properly a relic of the old Dualistic leaven, which sees in evil the resistless play, the unconquerable energy of an eternal principle; which refers it to a power that, could it have existed, would have made God impossible.

No. There must be no tampering with the idea and character of God; with His Unity, with His Omnipotence, with His Sanctity. To deny these is to destroy, in human thought, the ascertained object of religion. If there is one God, All-powerful and moral, and if moral evil is a fact in the universe, the existence and nature of moral evil must be in some way accounted for by serious Theists, if it can be accounted for at all, without impugning the morality and the Omnipotence of God.

II.

What, then, is sin in itself? What representation of it will neither obliterate the lines of moral truth, nor do injustice to the Sanctity or the Omnipotence of God?

S. James, in the passage which is before us, furnishes us with materials for answering this question. He says that desire when it hath conceived bringeth forth sin. He thus places the origin of moral evil in the created will, of which desire is the moral ingredient. Desire is, indeed, the raw material of moral life. It is the plastic force which may become, under different circumstances, either sanctity or sin: and thus S. Augustine has defined virtue as "love or desire ruled by true order." Desire is part of the original outfit of every human being; a sympathetic force by which the various instincts and faculties of our nature are drawn towards a something external to itself. What is that something? In man's unfallen state of old, and in his state of perfectly restored sanctity hereafter, God is the true object of all human desires: man desires God for His own sake, and all created objects only for the sake of God. In the original design of God, desire in the moral world corresponds to the law of attraction in the physical; and the perfected saint, in all the activity of his moral and intellectual life, moves around the great Centre of his adoration with an undeviating regularity, such as is that of the planet circling in its orbit around its parent sun. But the planet cannot modify or weaken the attraction which governs it. It cannot plunge anarchically through space, seeking a place in some other system where it may move around some other sun, or itself become the centre of other satellites; whereas desire, being moral, does not bind free agents to loyal revolutions around their true Centre by any such necessity. Man may at his option cease to desire God: he may, in the stead of God, desire one of God's creatures for its own sake, and with the vehemence of an absorbing passion.[1] And since no other creature can really take God's place, man thus comes to make himself his own centre; to view all persons and events relatively to himself; to think of God, if at all, as only one of the points on the circumference of his own petty and fictitious universe. When desire is thus perverted, by being wedded to the things of time and sense, as if they could really satisfy the yearnings of the soul, it "bringeth forth sin." Like an atmosphere charged with infection, desire spent upon created things is pregnant with sin: it implies that idolatrous surrender of self to creatures, that passionate claim upon creatures on behalf of self, which in the end

1 S. John ii. 17, ἐπιθυμία τοῦ κόσμου. Tit. ii. 12; Rom. vii. 7, 8.

breaks the bond between God and the soul.[1] And hence an act, or series of acts, whether of thought, or word, or deed, to which in its freedom the will consents, and which contradict the moral order of the universe.

And this is sin. Sin, to be complete, need not become speech or action: a formed desire, deliberately assented to by the will, constitutes sin. "He that looketh on a woman," says our Lord, "to desire her, hath committed adultery with her already in his heart."[2] Indeed, it is the internal act, and not the material product of the act, which is chiefly of moral importance. What is the precise form or turn of the inward act? Here the beautiful and suggestive words, which are used to express the idea of sin in the sacred language, but which are untranslateable into our clumsier Western tongue, will help us. In the fifty-first Psalm, for instance, besides the generic expression for evil,[3] there are three words which describe different aspects of the idea of sin. Of these, one implies that God's will being the aim which man rightly pursues, sin is a missing his true goal in life.[4] A second regards

[1] This aspect of sin has been well re-stated in Jul. Müller's Lehr. v. d. Sünde, i. i. c. 3.

[2] S. Matt. v. 28.

[3] רַע, v. 6, broadly opposed to טוֹב—Gen. xxiv. 50; Levit. xxvii. 10. In a more emphatic moral sense, Prov. viii. 13; Ps. vii. 10. רָשָׁע means originally to be noisy, tempestuous; the transition to the idea of moral disorder appears in רָעַע, which is primarily used of breaking in pieces with a crash, Job xxxiv. 24, Ps. ii. 9; then of evil generally, and finally, in the Hiphil especially, of evil action.—J. Müller, Lehr. v. d. Sünde, i. i. c. 2.

[4] חָטָא, v. 5. The primary idea seems to be that of stumbling on the way to a goal—Prov. xix. 2; in which is implied the missing of the object of

sin as a twisting or perversion of the will from the right way.[1] A third brands it as rebellious transgression of Divine law,[2] of a covenant with God, of the law which man is bound to obey. The New Testament expressions substantially correspond; and they have *this* in common. Sin is an offence against moral truth; known, and contradicted although known. "Sin," says S. Augustine, "is something said or done or desired in contradiction to the Eternal Law."

Why the "Eternal" Law? This question can only be answered when we reflect on the nature of moral truth. Moral truth is not like the laws and facts of the physical world; it is not something which might have been otherwise than as it is, had God so willed. God was under no necessity to make either one or a million suns or planets, or to furnish them with a particular temperature and particular inhabitants. Why not? Because there was nothing in His necessary nature which constrained Him to do so. He created in His freedom: He created as He created in His freedom: He might have created otherwise: He was free not to have created at all. But could God ever have sanctioned you or me in saying that that which

search—Prov. viii. 36. Not that חטא is used only or chiefly of sins of infirmity, whether of thought or will: it is often applied to the gravest sins, and implies that which is characteristic of all sin, namely, that sin is a moral action, in which man misses the aim for which he was created by God.

[1] עָוֹן, v. 4, from עָוָה, to be bent or distorted, implies evil considered as departure from man's appointed path.—Job. xiii. 26; Gen. iv. 13.

[2] פֶּשַׁע, v. 5. פָּשַׁע primarily implies faithless rebellion against a covenant, as in Isa. i. 2, xliii. 27; Jerem. iii. 13; Amos iv. 4; 1 Kings xii. 19, &c.

we know to be false is true? Why not? Because, in sanctioning us, God would be contradicting, not a law which He might have made other than as He has made it, but a necessary truth of His own eternal nature. A moral truth is like a mathematical axiom; we see it intuitively, and we do this because it is necessarily true, and as being necessarily true, is also a truth of God's eternal nature. Can any reasonable man, for instance, without destroying and uprooting the very constitution of the mind which God has given him, conceive that under any possible circumstances it could ever have been true that things which are equal to the same are not equal to one another? If not; then, here we have an Eternal Truth. And if this be an Eternal Truth, it is, as such, a real part of God's Eternal Nature; since if this be denied, we must admit that there are eternal truths independent of God, and existing eternally apart from Him. Would not this in effect be a denial of His solitary self-existence? Either God does not exist, or all that is eternal is God. But if pure mathematical truth, as being eternally true, be thus Divine, moral truth is not less so. If we cannot believe that a lie was ever right, this is because veracity is an eternal law of the Divine nature; and this applies to the whole moral law, which is, in reality, the Divine nature formulated into rules which suit the conditions of creaturely existence. Thus, given the parental relationship, it never could have been right to dishonour a father or a mother: given human life, murder could never have been other than criminal:

given the responsibility of transmitting the gift of life, and adultery, which trifles with that responsibility, could never have been condoned: given the idea of personal rights, of property, and stealing is necessarily condemned. And thus it is that sin does not contradict a rule which God has made of one kind, but which He might have made of another; it contradicts a rule which, in its principle, is necessary and eternal; a rule which does not depend even upon the will of God Himself, since it embodies and expresses His Divine and unchanging Nature; a rule which accordingly it is impossible to contradict, without running counter to, and, so far as we can, setting at naught and destroying the very being and nature of God Himself. "Against Thee only have I sinned," is the voice of the sinner's deepest knowledge of himself. And it was this which led ancient divines to say, that if, *per impossibile*, moral evil could be pushed to a point of sufficient exaggeration, it would annihilate God. By this saying, they expressed the vital and fundamental antagonism which exists between sin and the Divine nature.

Now, such an account of moral evil cannot be said to attenuate its malignity; but is it equally careful of the character of God? If evil be thus antagonistic to God, how can God, at once Almighty and All-holy, have allowed it to exist? As All-holy, He must abhor it; as Almighty, He surely might have proscribed what He abhors?

The answer is, that, notwithstanding the inherent quality of evil, the possibility of its existence is, so far as we can see, a needful condition of true moral freedom. God might have created a universe ruled from first to last by physical law, and so incapable of deviation from the true rule of its action. In such an universe, moral evil would have found no place, only because there would have been no creatures properly capable of moral good. Our experience tells us that God has not chosen to stint down His creative activity to these proportions: that we are free agents, is not more a matter of faith, than of experience. We know that God has created beings whose high privilege it is to be able freely to choose Him as their king, as the accepted Master of their whole inward life; but if this privilege is to be real, it also carries with it the implied power of rejecting Him. The alternative risk is the inevitable condition of the consummate honour: it is actually a substantial part of the honour. A moral being must at least have a capacity for disobedience if he is to be able freely to obey.

If, then, God has permitted evil, it is not because He has ceased to be Himself, but because His generosity has been abused. The source and root of moral evil is to be found, not in the Good God, but in the abused freedom of the creature, whether it be man or angel. It were hard indeed to blaspheme God for His generosity; to complain that He has made us men and not brutes or stones, because, forsooth, as a race, as well as in our individual lives, we have turned His bounty against Himself, and made the greatness of His gift the measure of our degradation.

It will be urged that God must have "foreseen" the

abuse that would follow upon His gift of freedom. Certainly. But those who believe in His wisdom and His love at all, must surely believe that He foresaw much else. They will believe with S. Paul that if, in the event, sin has abounded, grace has much more abounded.[1] They will believe with S. Augustine that "God knew it to be more agreeable to His almighty goodness even to bring good out of evil, than not to permit evil to exist."[2] He might be trusted to strike the balance of advantages between a universe ruled only by physical law and a universe so open to the possible invasion of evil as to be darkened by its actual presence and apparent victory, but withal illuminated by the remedy, which, in the long run, was to be much more than equal to grappling with the disease. Sin might be tolerated, if the Eternal Son was to redeem the world. We know at any rate how the world's Ruler has decided, and it is scarcely reasonable to complain that He has not admitted us to share all the reasons which governed His decision.

III.

Here, then, I repeat the statement with which I began, that if a religion is to be real life-controlling power, it

[1] Rom. v. 18, 19, 20, *οὗ δὲ ἐπλεόνασεν ἡ ἁμαρτία, ὑπερεπερίσσευσεν ἡ χάρις.*

[2] De Cor. et Gr. c. 10. Qui creavit omnia bona valde et mala ex bonis exoritura esse præscivit; scivit magis ad omnipotentissimam suam bonitatem pertinere etiam de malis benefacere quam mala esse non sinere.

must practically recognize the fact of sin. For, since sin provokes God's necessary displeasure on the one hand, and destroys man's power and even his wish to seek God on the other, its direct effect is to break up that bond between God and man in which religion essentially consists. Religion, therefore, must deal with sin, not as if it were making a supererogatory exertion, but as a condition of its own existence. It must remove this fatal obstacle to its proper activity, if it is to exist at all. Not less necessary is this practical recognition of sin by religion, if religion is to be of any real benefit to society. Go out into the streets of this great capital, or read the daily journals which register the thought and incidents of our national life, and what are the two spectres which meet you most constantly? Are they not suffering and crime? And what is suffering, at least in the main, but the effect and shadow of sin; if not of the sufferer's own sin, yet at least of some physical or social legacy from a parent's error? What is crime in its most venial form, but sin, prompted by suffering and organized and solidified, until in its brutal exuberance it threatens even the existence of society? Has religion nothing to say to the moral mischief which is the parent of these dark phantoms? Is she dreaming? Is she powerless? Is she abandoning her high hope and mission of saving humanity from its worst enemies?

It is here that true religion parts company altogether with certain phases of so-termed religious thought, which are not without an ambition to be considered at least the rudiments of some future religion of civilization. Doubtless they embody much which recommends them, at any rate, to the interest of educated people. They are philosophical; they are enterprising; they are in good taste; they occupy a large amount of attention in our journals and periodicals. Nor are they insensible to the evil of crime, considered as a cause of social disturbance and danger. They would sometimes deal more hardly with it than would be morally possible for men who had a deeper insight into the relative responsibility of criminals. But ignoring the awful yet blessed doctrines of Redemption and Grace, they have no remedy for sin; no remedy, that is, of any practical value; and after all, sin is the great fact with which they ought to deal. Animated speculation on religious topics, careful reproduction of the external drapery of scenes in early sacred history, quick capacity for analyzing and delineating sentiment, is very welcome in its place. It has indisputably a literary value; but it does not help us to confront the stern realities of this human world. The religion which has no fixed doctrines, or scarcely any; no code of absolute truth, to be taught and suffered for at all costs; no word of heart-searching warning, and yet of tenderest consolation for sinners,—is not really a religion at all. It is at best a very one-sided philosophy. Its endeavours to deal with the great heart-sores of humanity remind us of some great physician who, at the bedside of a patient, writhing in protracted agony, should airily discuss his own last excursion in the Alps, or the last debate in Parliament, or at best the most recent resolution arrived at by the Metropolitan Board of Health.

The religion of Jesus Christ, as taught by His Apostles, does not thus trifle with the seriousness of sin. It begins by deepening the sense of sin, the perception of its real area and power in human life. It adds poignancy to the feeling of shame and guilt which follows upon deliberate sinful action in a healthy conscience. By the Mosaic law there was a knowledge of sin.[1] By the teaching and example of Jesus Christ there is a much truer and deeper knowledge of it.[2] That faultless and unapproached Life which we study in the pages of the Gospels, brought home to the heart as well as to the understanding by the secret teaching of the Eternal Spirit, endows the Christian with an ideal of sanctity altogether his own.[3] Around the Sermon on the Mount, or the last discourse in the supper-room, there is an unearthly atmosphere of purity and holiness, which lights up in the soul, with microscopic distinctness, the consciousness of secret evil, more perfectly than could any code of precepts. One only appearing among us in human form has been able to ask the tremendous question, "Which of you convinceth Me of sin?"[4] And as we gaze on Him, holy, harmless, undefiled, separate from sinners, in His purity, His courage, His humility, His tenderness, His majestic moral strength, His fearless loyalty to truth, His vast charity, we see that which reveals us to ourselves. At the feet of the Lamb without blemish and immaculate, we feel,

[1] Rom. iii. 20. [2] S. Matt. v. 21-48. [3] S. John viii. 12. [4] S. John viii. 46.

with Job, that the report of God's sanctity has been at length exchanged for sight;[1] we exclaim with the Apostle, "Depart from me, for I am a sinful man, O Lord."[2]

Nor does Jesus Christ stop here. He reveals, as does no other, not merely the fact and malignity of sin, but its consequences. The sternest things that have ever been said, as regards sin's prospects in another world, first passed the tenderest lips that ever proclaimed God's love to man.[3] Our Lord would not leave the revelation of the penal future to His Apostles: He took the unpopularity of making such a revelation upon Himself. No unbelieving criticism can really touch the plain meaning of the tremendous words in which the All-Merciful One has depicted the case of a moral being, stiffened by final impenitence into a permanent self-torturing rebellion against Eternal Justice and Eternal Love. But for that awful measure of sin, the saying concerning Judas had been a paradox; "It were good for that man if he had never been born." [4]

Yet if Jesus Christ had only taught us the penalties of sin, He would but have enhanced the terrors of the ancient law. Whereas, in reality, He has made it possible for us to look at moral evil as it is. We Christians can dare to face it, for He has brought us both a pardon and an antidote. His cross and passion are a revelation as well as a cure. When dying, He shews us what sin is. At least to those who take Him at His word, and see in Him One Higher

[1] Job xlii. 5. [2] S. Luke v. 8.
[3] S. Mark ix. 43-48; S. Matt. xxv. 46; S. John v. 29.
[4] S. Matt. xxvi. 24; S. Mark xiv. 21.

than the sons of men, the Cross will surely have this meaning. Why could not the Holy One, manifested to His reasonable creatures in a form of sense, have ended a life of beneficence and glory by such a visible ascent to heaven as was that of the Tishbite? Why those years of privation and sorrow, those sufferings and insults, that shame and scorn? Why the prostration in the garden, and the Wounds and the Blood, and the agony lengthened out by ingenious cruelty, and the ostentatious exultation and triumph of the hosts of evil, and the darkness and gloom of the closing scene? Would not this mean failure, if it had not been proved by the event to mean a victory, wherein the Divine Sufferer was triumphing, as His Apostle notes, over the associated powers of darkness?[1] That unfathomed pain is the true measure of sin for Christians. In that keen sensitiveness, in that strength of a self-sacrificing Will, in that exhaustive anticipation of and intellectual familiarity with the coming Agony, followed by so entire an acceptance of it, we Christians discern the real character of the adversary which the Perfect Moral Being conquered by His voluntary death. From that fountain of pardon and strength which He opened upon Calvary, all[2] the resources which His Church can wield in her struggle with His great enemy, and in her continuation of His work of reconciliation and peace, are consistently derived. No virtue exists in the world which is not His; no cleansing which His Blood has not made good. Standing beneath the Cross, we can never

[1] Col. ii. 15. [2] Acts iv. 12.

deem moral evil less or other than the greatest, if it be not rather the only evil. Kneeling before the Crucified, be our sense of guilt what it may, we can never despair; since the complete revelation of the malignity of sin is also and simultaneously a revelation of the Love that knows no bounds.[1]

It is these concrete truths, and no abstract considerations, which really keep alive in the Christian heart an abhorrence and dread of moral evil. With that evil, even when all has been pardoned, every Christian life is, from first to last, in varying degrees, a struggle. There are great conflicts, and there are periods of comparative repose; there are days of failure as well as days of victory; there are quickenings of buoyant thankful hope, and there are hours of a discouragement which is only not despair. But two things a genuine Christian never does. He never makes light of any known sin,[2] and he never admits it to be invincible.[3] While he constantly endeavours, by the sanctification of his desires, by entwining his affections more and more around the Source of goodness, to destroy sin in the bud, or rather in its root and principle, he is never off his guard; never surprised at new proofs of his natural weakness; never disposed to underrate either his dangers or his strength. He knows that now, as eighteen centuries ago, he wrestles not against flesh and blood,[4] but against principalities and powers that bear him no good will: he

[1] 2 Cor. v. 14; Rom. v. 15.
[2] 1 S. John iii. 9; v. 18.
[3] 1 Cor. x. 12.
[4] Eph. vi. 12.

knows, that as at the first so now, "if any man sin, we have an Advocate with the Father, Jesus Christ the righteous, and He is the propitiation for our sins."[1] And thus, in his inmost life, he is at once anxious and hopeful; confident yet without presumption; alive to all that is at stake day by day, hour by hour; yet stayed upon the thought, nay, upon the felt presence of a Love Which has not really left him to himself. And at last, when it seems best to that Eternal Love, the day of struggle draws to its close,[2] and the towers of the Everlasting City come into view; the city within whose precincts intellectual error cannot penetrate, and moral failure is unknown. "Thanks be to God Who giveth us the victory through our Lord Jesus Christ."[3]

Your alms are asked to-day on behalf of the additional clergy needed by this great parish with its twenty thousand poor.[4] You will feel that this is an opportunity of testing the earnestness of your desire to struggle against our common enemy, whether in the world or in your own hearts, by freely placing your means at His disposal, Who is its only real Conqueror.

[1] 1 S. John ii. 1. [2] 2 Tim. iv. 6. [3] 1 Cor. xv. 57.
[4] St. James's, Piccadilly, Additional Curates' Fund.

LECTURE V.

Fifth Sunday in Lent.

PRAYER, THE CHARACTERISTIC ACTION OF RELIGION.

S. MATT. vii. 7.

Ask and it shall be given you.

RELIGION is the bond between the soul and God, which sin, by virtue of its very nature, breaks up and destroys. It is of importance to inquire whether man can strengthen and intensify that which he can, it seems, so easily ruin if he will. Does his power lie only in the direction of destruction? Has he no means of invigorating and repairing a tie, in itself so precious, yet in some respects so frail? The answer lies in our Lord's promise. Prayer is the act by which man, conscious at once of his weakness and of his immortality, puts himself into real and effective communication with the Almighty, the Eternal, the Self-Existent God. I say, effective communication. For prayer, as our Lord teaches in the text and elsewhere, is not without results. God answers prayer in many ways. His answers to the soul's petition for health and strength are collectively described as grace; grace being the invisible influence whereby He on His part strengthens and quickens the tie which binds the petitioner to Himself. "Ask and it shall be given you." Prayer then braces the bond of religion from the side of man; and grace, God's highest answer to prayer, braces it in a different and far more powerful sense on the part of God.

It is not too much to say that the practice of prayer is co-extensive with the idea of religion. Wherever man has believed a higher power to exist, he has not merely discussed the possibility of entering into converse with such a power; he has assumed, as a matter of course, that he can do so. Upon desert plains and wild promontories, not less than in crowded thoroughfares and gorgeous temples, priesthoods, and kings, and multitudes have taken prayer for granted, as being the most practical as well as the most interesting and solemn concern of life. The surface of the earth, of parts of our own island, is still covered with the relics of some among these ancient worships. And if the implied conceptions of deity were degraded, and the rites cruel, or inhuman, or impure, and the minds of the worshippers not seldom imbruted by the very acts which should have raised them heavenward; still the idea of worship as the natural correlative of belief in the superhuman was always there. To know that a higher Being existed, and interested Himself, in whatever way, in the destinies of man, was to feel that it was at once a right and a duty to approach Him.

And as we pass the historical lines within which, as Christians believe, mankind has enjoyed a knowledge of God's successive revelations of His true self and His true will, we find that prayer is the prominent feature, the characteristic exercise of man's highest life. Sacrifice begins at the very gates of Eden.[1] The life of early Patriarchs is described as a "walking with God," a continuous reference of thought and aspiration to the Father above, Who yet was so near them.[2] And after the Mosaic Law was given, when the idea and range of sin had been deepened and extended in the mind of Israel, we find prayer organized in a system of sacrifices, suited to various wants and moods of the human soul, consciously dealing with its God as the King, both of the sacred nation and of the individual conscience. Penitence, thanksgiving, intercession, adoration, each found an appropriate expression.[3] Later still, in the Psalter, prayer—the purest, the loftiest, the most passionate—took shape in imperishable forms. And when at length a new revelation was made in Jesus Christ, there was little to add to what was already believed as to the power and obligation of prayer, beyond revealing the secret of its acceptance. Our Lord's precepts[4] and example[5] are sufficiently emphatic; and His Apostles appear to represent prayer not so much as a practice of

[1] Gen. iv. 4. [2] Gen. v. 24; vi. 9. [3] Levit. i.-vii.

[4] S. Matt. vi. 9; S. Luke xi. 2; S. Matt. xxvi. 41; S. Mark xi. 24; S. Luke xviii. 1, &c.

[5] S. Matt. xiv. 23; S. Mark vi. 46; S. Luke vi. 12, ix. 28; S. John xvii. 1.

the Christian life, as its very breath and instinctive movement. The Christian must be "continuing instant in prayer;" he must "pray without ceasing."[1]

I.

Each faculty, or endowment, or form of activity that belongs to man has, over and above a number of more indirect effects, its appropriate and characteristic action, in which its whole strength is embarked, and in which it has, so to speak, its full play. To this law religion is no exception. While its influence upon human life is strong and various in proportion to its high aim and object; while it is felt, when it wields real empire, in every department of human activity and interest, as an invigorating, purifying, chastening, restraining, guiding influence, it too has a work peculiarly its own. In this work it is wont, if we may so speak, to embark its collective forces, and to become peculiarly conscious of its direction and intensity. This work is prayer. Prayer is emphatically religion in action. It is the soul of man engaging in that particular form of activity which presupposes the existence of a great bond between itself and God. Prayer is, therefore, nothing else or less than the noblest kind of human exertion. It

[1] Rom. xii. 12; 1 Thess. v. 17.

is the one department of action in which man realizes the highest privilege and capacity of his being. And, in doing this, he is himself enriched and ennobled almost indefinitely: now, as of old, when he comes down from the mountain, his face bears tokens of an irradiation which is not of this world.

That this estimate of the value of prayer is not universal among educated people in our day, is only too notorious. If many a man were to put into words with perfect honesty and explicitness what he thinks, he would say that prayer is an excellent thing for a clergyman, or for a recluse, or for a sentimentalist, or for women and children generally; that it has its uses as a form of desultory occupation, an outlet for feeling, a means of discipline. For himself, he cannot really think that much prayer would help him much. It implies a life of feeling—perhaps, he would say, of morbid feeling; and he prides himself upon being guided only by reflection. It is sustained, he thinks, by imagination, rather than by reason; and he deems imagination puerile and feminine. His religion, whatever it is, has nothing to do with imagination, and is hard reason from first to last; and accordingly prayer seems to him to be altogether less worthy of the energies of a thinking man than hard work, whether it be work of the hands or of the brains, whether it be study or business. The dignity of real labour is proverbial, but where, he asks, is the dignity of so sentimental an occupation as prayer? "For his own part, he thinks," (I am quoting words which have actually been used) "that religion is not worship, but only another name for doing good to our fellow-creatures."

Now, without saying one word to disparage the intimate connection between religion and philanthropy, let us examine the idea of prayer, which is taken for granted in such language as the foregoing. Is it true that prayer is, as is assumed, little else than the half passive play of sentiment which flows languidly on through the minutes or hours of easy reverie? Let those who have really prayed give the answer. They sometimes describe prayer with the patriarch Jacob as a wrestling together with an Unseen Power, which may last, not unfrequently in an earnest life, late into the night hours, or even to the break of day.[1] Sometimes they refer to common intercession with S. Paul as a concerted struggle.[2] They have, when praying, their eyes fixed upon the Great Intercessor in Gethsemane, upon the drops of blood which fall to the ground in that Agony of Resignation and Sacrifice.[3] Importunity is of the essence of successful prayer. Our Lord's references to the subject especially imply this. The Friend who is at rest with his family, will rise at last to give a loaf to the hungry applicant.[4] The Unjust Judge yields in the end to the resistless eagerness of the widow's cry.[5] Our Lord's blessing on the Syro-Phœnician woman is the consecration of importunity with God.[6] And importunity means, not dreaminess, but sustained work. It is through prayer especially that "the

[1] Gen. xxxii. 24. [2] Rom. xv. 30. [3] S. Luke xxii. 44. [4] S. Luke xi. 8.
[5] S. Luke xviii. 5. [6] S. Matt. xv. 27-28; S. Mark vii. 28-29.

kingdom of heaven suffereth violence, and the violent take it by force."[1] It was a saying of the late Bishop Hamilton of Salisbury, that "no man was likely to do much good in prayer who did not begin by looking upon it in the light of a work, to be prepared for and persevered in with all the earnestness which we bring to bear upon subjects which are, in our opinion, at once most interesting and most necessary."

This indeed will appear, if, looking to an act of real prayer, we take it to pieces. Of what does it consist? It consists always of three separate forms of activity which, in the case of different persons, co-exist in very varying degrees of intensity, but which are found, in some degree, in all who pray, whenever they pray.

To pray, is first of all to put the understanding in motion, and to direct it upon the Highest Object to Which it can possibly address itself, the Infinite God. In our private prayers, as in our public liturgies, we generally preface the petition itself by naming one or more of His attributes. Almighty and Everlasting God! If the understanding is really at work at all, how overwhelming are the ideas, the truths, which pass thus before it; a boundless Power, an Existence which knows neither beginning nor end. Then the substance of the petition, the motives which are alleged for urging it, the issues which depend upon its being granted or being refused, present themselves to the eye of the understanding. And if our Lord Jesus Christ is not Him-

[1] S. Matt. xi. 12.

self, as being both God and Man, the object of prayer, yet His perpetual and prevailing intercession opens upon Christian thought the inmost mysteries before the Eternal Throne. And thus any common act of real prayer keeps, not the imagination, but the understanding, occupied earnestly, absorbingly, under the guidance of faith, from first to last.[1]

Next, to pray is to put the affections in motion: it is to open the heart. The object of prayer is the Uncreated Love, the Eternal Beauty; He of Whose beauty all that moves love and admiration here is at best a pale reflection. To be in His presence in prayer, is to be conscious of an expansion of the heart, and of the pleasure which accompanies it, which we feel, in another sense, when speaking with an intimate and loved friend or relative. And this movement of the affections is sustained throughout the act of prayer. It is invigorated by the spiritual sight of God, but it is also the original impulse which leads us to draw near to Him.[2] In true prayer as in teaching, "out of the abundance of the heart the mouth speaketh."[3]

Once more, to pray, is to put the will in motion, just as decidedly as we do when we sit down to read hard, or to walk up a steep hill against time.[4] That sovereign power in the soul, which we name the will, does not

[1] Eph. vi. 18; S. John iv. 22-29; Rom. x. 14; Heb. xi. 6.
[2] S. Matt. xv. 8; 1 S. John iii. 21-22.
[3] S. Matt. xii. 34; S. Luke vi. 45.
[4] S. John ix. 31; S. Matt. vii. 21; S. James iv. 7-8. These passages all imply that prayer in which the will is not engaged is worthless.

merely, in prayer, impel us to make the first necessary mental effort, but enters most penetratingly and vitally into the very action of the prayer itself. It is the will which presses the petition; it is the will which struggles with the reluctance of sloth or with the oppositions of passion; it is the will which perseveres; it is the will which exclaims, "I will not let Thee go, except Thou bless me."[1] The amount of will which we severally carry into the act of prayer is the ratio of its sincerity; and where prayer is at once real and prolonged, the demands which it makes upon our power of concentrating determination into a specific and continuous act are very considerable indeed.

Now, these three ingredients of prayer are also ingredients in all real work, whether of the brains or of the hands. The sustained effort of the intelligence and of the will must be seconded in work no less than in prayer by a movement of the affections, if work is to be really successful. A man must love his work to do it well. The difference between prayer and ordinary work is that in prayer the three ingredients are more equally balanced. Study may in time become intellectual habit, which scarcely demands any effort of will: handiwork may in time become so mechanical as to require little or no guidance from thought: each may exist in a considerable, although not in the highest degree of excellence, without any co-operation of the affections. Not so prayer. It is always the joint act of the will

[1] Gen. xxxii. 26.

and the understanding, impelled by the affections; and when either will or intelligence is wanting, prayer at once ceases to be itself, by degenerating into a barren intellectual exercise, or into a mechanical and unspiritual routine.

The dignity of prayer as being real work becomes clear to us if we consider the faculties which it employs. This will be made clearer still if we consider the effect of all sincere prayer upon the habitual atmosphere of the soul. Prayer places the soul face to face with facts of the first order of solemnity and importance; with its real self, and with its God. And just as art, or study, or labour in any department is elevating, when it takes us out of and beyond the petty range of daily and perhaps material interests, while yet it quickens interest in them by kindling higher enthusiasms into life; so in a peculiar and transcendent sense it is with prayer. Prâyer is man's inmost movement towards a Higher Power; but what is the intellectual view or apprehension of himself that originally impels him to move? Under what aspect does man appear to himself in prayer? In a former lecture we have encountered the mystery which lies enclosed within each one of us,—the mystery which is yet a fact,—of an undying personality. It is that which each human speaker describes as "I." It is that of which each of us is conscious as no one else can be conscious. Its existence is not proved to us by a demonstration, since we apprehend it as immediately obvious. Its certainty can be shaken by no sophistical or destructive argument, since our conviction of its reality is based upon a continuous act of primary perception. No sooner do we withdraw ourselves from the importunities of sense, from the wanderings of imagination, from the misleading phrases which confuse the mental sight, than we find ourselves face to face with this fact, represented by "I." For it is neither the body which the real self may ignore, nor a passionate impulse which the real self may conquer, nor even that understanding which, close as it is to the real self, is yet distinct from it. The body may be in its decrepitude; the flames of passion may have died away; the understanding may be almost in its dotage; yet the inward, self-possessed, self-governing being may remain untouched, realizing itself in struggling against the instincts of bodily weakness, and in crushing out the embers which survive the fires of extinct passions. Now it is this self, conscious of its greatness, conscious of its weakness, which is the real agent in prayer. In its oppressive sense of solitude, even in the midst of multitudes, this self longs to go forth, and to commune with the Father of spirits Who gave it life. This real self it is which apprehends God with the understanding, which embraces Him with the affections, which resolves through the will to obey Him; and thus does it underlie and unite the complex elements of prayer, so that in true heartfelt prayer we become so conscious of its vitality and power. It is in prayer especially that we cease to live, as it were, in a single faculty, or on the surface of our being: it is in prayer that we cease to regard ourselves as animal forms, or as social powers, or as family characters and look hard, for the time being, at ourselves, as being what we really are; that is to say, as immortal spirits, outwardly draped in social forms and proprieties, and linked to a body of flesh and blood, but in our felt spiritual solitude looking steadily upwards at the face of God, and straining our eyes onwards towards the great eternity which lies before us.[1]

Prayer is then so noble, because it is the work of man as man; of man realizing his being and destiny with a vividness which is necessary to him in no other occupation. But what shall we say of it, when we reflect further that in prayer man holds converse with God: that the Being of Beings, with all His majestic attributes, filling and transcending the created universe, traversing human history, traversing each man's own individual history, is before him: that although man is dust and ashes, he is, by prayer, already welcomed in the very courts of heaven? It is not necessary to dwell on this topic. Whatever be the daily occupations of any in this Church, be he a worker with the hands or a worker with the brain, be he gentle or simple, be he unlettered or educated, be he high in the state or among the millions at its base, is it not certain that the nobleness of his highest forms of labour must fall infinitely below that of any single human spirit entering consciously into converse with the Infinite and Eternal God?

[1] S. Luke xviii. 13, 14.

II.

But granted, men say, the dignity of prayer—granted even its dignity as labour: what if this labour be misapplied? There are many functions in many states, very dignified and not a little onerous, yet in a social and human sense not very productive. Is prayer, in its sphere, of this description? Has it no tangible results? Does it end with itself? Can the labourer in this field point to anything definite that is achieved by his exertions?

The question is sufficiently serious at all times, but especially in our own positive and practical day. And it is necessary to make two observations, that we may see more clearly what issue is precisely before us.

In the first place, there is here no question as to the subjective effect of prayer; the effect which it confessedly has upon the mind and character of the person who prays. Such effects have been admitted on the part of those who unhappily do not pray themselves; just as the Jews, at the time of the Betrayal, were so alive to tokens in the disciples of companionship with Jesus. That all the effects of Christian prayer upon the soul, or most of them, are natural, a Christian cannot admit: he believes them to be chiefly due to the transforming power of the grace of God, given, as at other times, so especially in answer to prayer. But that *some* effects of prayer upon the soul are natural consequences of directing the mind and the affections towards a superhuman object, whether real or ideal, may be fully granted. Thus it has been observed that persons without natural ability have, through the earnestness of their devotional habits, acquired in time powers of sustained thought, and an accuracy and delicacy of intellectual touch, which would not else have belonged to them. The intellect being the instrument by which the soul handles religious truth, a real interest in religious truth will of itself often furnish an educational discipline; it alone educates an intellect which would otherwise be uneducated.[1] The moral effects of devotion are naturally more striking and abundant. Habitual prayer constantly confers decision on the wavering, and energy on the listless, and calmness on the excitable, and disinterestedness on the selfish. It braces the moral nature by transporting it into a clear, invigorating unearthly atmosphere: it builds up the moral life, insensibly but surely remedying its deficiencies, and strengthening its weak points, till there emerges a comparatively symmetrical and consistent whole, the excellence of which all must admit, though its secret is known only to those who know it by experience.[2] Akin to the moral are the social effects of prayer. Prayer makes men as members of society different in their whole bearing from those who do not pray. It gilds social intercourse and conduct with a tenderness, an unobtrusiveness, a sincerity, a frankness, an evenness of temper, a cheerfulness, a collectedness, a con-

[1] Ps. cxix. 100. [2] Ps. xxvii. 4, 5, 6.

stant consideration for others, united to a simple loyalty to truth and duty, which leavens and strengthens society. Nay, it is not too much to say that prayer has even physical results. The countenance of a Fra Angelico reflects his spirit no less than does his art: the bright eye, the pure elevated expression, speak for themselves. It was said of one who has died within the present generation,[1] that in his later years his face was like that of an illuminated clock; the colour and gilding had long faded away from the hands and figures, but the ravages of time were more than compensated for by the light which shone from within. This was what might have been expected in an aged man of great piety; to have lived in spirit on Mount Tabor during the years of a long life is to have caught in its closing hours some rays of the glory of the Transfiguration.

Secondly, prayer is not only—perhaps in some of the holiest souls it is not even chiefly—a petition for something that we want and do not possess. In the larger sense of the word, as the spiritual language of the soul, prayer is intercourse with God, often seeking no end beyond the pleasure of such intercourse. It is praise; it is congratulation; it is adoration of the Infinite Majesty; it is a colloquy in which the soul engages with the All-wise and the All-holy; it is a basking in the sunshine, varied by ejaculations of thankfulness to the Sun of Righteousness for His light and His warmth. In this

[1] Rev. J. Keble.

larger sense, the earlier part of the Te Deum is prayer as much as the latter part; the earliest and latest clauses of the Gloria in Excelsis as truly as the central ones; the Sanctus or the Jubilate no less than the Litany; the Magnificat as certainly as the fifty-first Psalm. When we seek the company of our friends, we do not seek it simply with the view of getting something from them: it is a pleasure to be with them, to be talking to them at all, or about anything; to be in possession of their sympathies and to be shewing our delight at it; to be assuring them of their place in our hearts and thoughts. So it is with the soul, when dealing with the Friend of friends—with God. Prayer is not, as it has been scornfully described, "only a machine warranted by theologians to make God do what His clients want:" it is a great deal more than petition, which is only one department of it: it is nothing less than the whole spiritual action of the soul turned towards God as its true and adequate object. And if used in this comprehensive sense, it is clear that, as to much prayer, in the sense of spiritual intercourse with God, the question whether it is answered can never arise, for the simple reason that no answer is asked for.

But whether prayer means only, as in popular language it does generally mean, petition for a specific object, or the whole cycle of possible communion between the soul and God, the question whether it is heard is a very practical one. We do not address inanimate objects, however beautiful they may be, except in the way of poetical apostrophe. We do not enter into spiritual colloquy with the mountains, or the rivers, or the skies, with a view to discharging a duty to them, or really improving ourselves.[1] If there is really no being above who does hear us, what can be the use of continuing a practice that is based upon an altogether false presumption? The subjective benefits of prayer depend upon our belief in its real power. But even if they did not, who would go through a confessedly fictitious exercise at regular intervals with a view to securing them? Who would continue to pray regularly, if he were once well persuaded that the effect of prayer is after all only like the effect of the higher philosophy or poetry; an education and a stimulus to the soul of man, but not an influence that can really touch the mind or will of that Being to Whom it is addressed? Nobody denies the moral and mental stimulus which is to be gained from the study of the great poets. But do we read Homer, or Shakespeare, or Goethe each morning and evening, and perhaps at the middle of the day? Or if such were the practice of any of us, should we have any approach to a feeling of being guilty of a criminal omission, if now and then we omitted to read them? No: if prayer is to be persevered in, it must be on the strength of a conviction that it is actually heard by a Living Person. We cannot practise any intricate trickery upon ourselves with a view to our moral edification. We cannot

[1] The apostrophes of the Psalms and the Benedicite are really acts of praise to God, of which His creatures furnish the occasion.

pray, if we believe in our hearts that in prayer we are only holding communion with an ideal world of our own creation; that we are like children, with overheated imaginations, vainly endeavouring to pass the barriers which really confine us to our dark earthly prison-house; while, in our failure, we half consciously, half unconsciously, cheat ourselves with the consolation of talking to shapes of power or benevolence traced by our fathers or by ourselves upon its inexorable walls. We cannot fall into the ranks of the Christian Church, lifting up the holy hands of sacrifice and intercession on all the mountains of the world, if in our hearts we see in her only a new company of Baal-worshippers gathering upon the slopes of some modern Carmel, and vainly endeavouring to rouse her idol into an impossible animation; while the Elijahs of materialistic science stand by to mock her fruitless efforts with the playful scorn of that tranquil irony to which their higher knowledge presumably entitles them.

The question whether God hears prayer, is at bottom the question whether He is really alive; whether in any true sense of the term He exists at all. No word is used more equivocally than the word "God" in the present day. If by "God" we mean only a product of the thought or consciousness of man, to which it cannot be certainly presumed that any being actually corresponds; the highest thought of man—yet only man's highest thought; then there is of course no one who can hear us. It has been said that if a man talks out loud to himself, apostrophizing what are in truth only his own conceptions, it is difficult not to credit him with a certain tinge of madness; and it would be just as practical to address our prayer to the carved and gilded idols of Babylon, whose manufacture roused the sternest satire of the Evangelical Prophet, as to the unreal abstractions, which, labelled with the Most Holy Name, are sent us from the intellectual workshops, ancient and modern, of Alexandria or of Berlin. And if by "God" is meant only the unseen force of the universe, or its collective forces; if He is the principle of growth in the plant, the life-principle in the animal or in man; we need not read Spinoza in order to convince ourselves of the fruitlessness of prayer. A self-existing force or cause, if such can be conceived, without intelligence, without personality, of course without any moral attributes, may be a thing to wonder at, but it certainly is not a being to speak to. We may of course ejaculate to such a thing if we like; but we might just as well say litanies to the winds or to the ocean. The question may be safely left to our utilitarian instincts. Time and strength, after all, are limited, and we shall not in the long run spend "our money," at least in this direction, "for that which is not bread, or our labour for that which satisfieth not."[1]

If, on the other hand, God exists, whether we think about Him or not; if He be not merely the mightiest force, the first of causes, but something more; if He be a personal Being, thinking with no limits to His thought, and willing

[1] Isaiah lv. 2.

with no fetters around His liberty; then surely we may reach Him, if we will. What is to prevent it? Cannot we men, at our pleasure, embody our thought, our feeling, our desires, or purposes in language, and so make them pass into and be apprehended by the created finite personalities around us? Where is the barrier that shall arrest thought, longings, desires, entreaties, not as yet clothed (why need they be clothed?) in speech, as they mount up from the soul towards the all-embracing Intelligence of God? And if God be not merely an infinite Intelligence, but a moral Being, a mighty Heart, so that justice, and mercy, and tenderness are attributes of His character, then to appeal to Him in virtue of these attributes is assuredly to appeal to Him to some purpose. If an Omnipresent Intelligence is a sufficient guarantee of His being able to hear us; an interest such as Justice and Mercy imply on His part towards creatures who depend upon Him for the original gift, and for the continued maintenance of life, is a guarantee of His willingness to do so.

It is on this ground that God is said to hear prayer in Holy Scripture. That He should do so follows from the reality of His nature as God. Elijah's irony implies that He is unlike the Phœnician Baal in being really alive.[1] A later Psalmist contrasts Him in like manner with the Assyrian idols, in that "they have eyes but see not, they have ears but hear not."[2] They do but fill their temples with gorgeous impotence. But Israel's God is the author

[1] 1 Kings xviii. 27. [2] Ps. cxv. 5.

of the very senses whereby we are conscious of each other's presence and wishes, and can enter into a companionship of thought and purpose. Is He debarred from the use of the gifts which He Himself bestows with so bountiful a hand? "He that planted the ear shall He not hear, or He that formed the eye shall He not see?"[1] Is it not, on the contrary, reasonable to believe that these powers must exist in a much higher and more perfect form in the one Being who gives them than in the myriads upon whom they are bestowed, and by whom they are only held in trust? And if it is improbable that, amid the innumerable beings who are alive to the sights and sounds of His creation, the Creator alone should be blind and deaf; is it more probable that He who has implanted in our breasts feelings of interest and pity for one another should be Himself insensible to our pain and need? Our hearts must anticipate and echo the statement of the Psalmist, that God does hear the desire of the poor; that the innocent, the oppressed, the suffering, have especial claims upon Him. And, to omit other illustrations, our Lord reveals Him as a Father, the common parent of men, of whose boundless love all earthly fatherhood is a shadow and a delegation. If the earthly parent, being evil, does not yet give a stone when his child cries for bread; the heavenly Father will not fall short of the teachings of an instinct which He has Himself implanted, by failing to give the Holy Spirit to them that ask Him.[2]

[1] Ps. xciv. 9. [2] S. Luke xi. 11-13.

III.

If a man is a good Theist—we need not say, a good Christian—he must believe that the Father of Spirits is not deaf to the voice of the human soul; that the thanksgiving and praise, the intercessions and supplications, the penitence and the self-surrender of beings to whom He has given moral and intellectual life, is not utterly lost upon the Giver. But will He indeed answer prayer, when prayer takes the form of a petition for some specific blessing which must be either granted or refused? There is no doubt as to the reply which the Bible and the Church have given to this question. But what do some modern thinkers say about it? Do they not deny the power of prayer, by surrounding the Throne of God with barriers, which, as they would have it, oblige Him, while "the sorrowful sighings of the prisoners" of this vale of tears incessantly "come before Him," to make as though He heard not, and to shorten His hand as if it could not save?"

The first presumed barrier against the efficacy of prayer to which men point is the scientific idea of law, reigning throughout the spiritual as well as the material universe. This idea, as we are constantly reminded, is one of the most remarkable conquests of modern thought; and no man, so it is said, can enter into it with an intelligent sympathy without abandoning the fond conceit that God will grant a particular favour to one of His creatures upon being asked to do so. It may have been pardonable to pray for rain, for health, for freedom from pestilence and famine, when these things were supposed to depend upon the caprice of an omnipotent will. But the scientific idea of law renders these prayers absurd. We know that a shower is the product of atmospheric laws, which make a shower, under certain circumstances, inevitable; that the death of an individual is the result of physiological laws which absolutely determine it. The idea that a shower or the death of a man are contingent upon the good pleasure of a Being Who can avert or precipitate them at pleasure is unscientific; it belongs to days when the idea of law had not yet dawned upon the intellect of civilization, or when, at any rate, large margins of the physical world, and the whole of the spiritual world, were supposed to be beyond its frontiers, as being abandoned to the government of a capricious omnipotence. Surely, it is added, we have really attained to a nobler idea of the universe, than was this old theological conception of the Bible and the Church: the superiority is to be measured by those fundamental instincts of fitness within us, which assign to law and order a higher place in our minds than can belong to a personal will.

Does not the very word law, by reason of its majestic and imposing associations, here involve us in some indistinctness of thought? What do we mean by law? When we speak of a law of nature are we thinking of some self-sustained invisible force, of which we can give no account except that here it is, a matter of experience? Or do we mean by a law of nature only a principle which, as our observation shews us, appears to govern particular actions of the Almighty Agent Who made and Who upholds the universe? If the former, let us frankly admit that we have not merely fettered God's freedom; we have, alas! ceased to believe in Him. For such self-sustained force is either self-originating, in which case there is no Being in existence who has made all that constitutes this universe. Or otherwise, having derived its first impact from the creative Will of God, this force has subsequently escaped altogether from His control, so that it now fetters His liberty; and, in this case, there is no Being in existence who is Almighty, in the sense of being really Master of this universe. If, however, we mean by law the observed regularity with which God works in nature as in grace; then, in our contact with law, we are dealing, not with a brutal, unintelligent, unconquerable force, but with the free will of an intelligent and moral Artist, Who works, in His perfect freedom, with sustained and beautiful symmetry. Where is the absurdity of asking Him to hold His hand, or to hasten His work? He to Whom we pray may be trusted to grant or to refuse a prayer, as may seem best to the highest wisdom and the truest love. And if He grant it, He is not without resources; even although we should have asked Him to suspend what we call a natural law. Can He not then provide for the freedom of His action without violating its order? Can He not supersede a lower rule of working by the intervention of a higher? If He really works at all; if something that is neither moral nor intelligent has not usurped His throne,—it is certain that "the thing that is done upon earth He doeth it Himself;" and that it is therefore as consistent with reason as with reverence to treat Him as being a free Agent, Who is not really tied and bound by the intellectual abstractions with which finite intellects would fain annihilate the freedom of His action.

No; to pray for rain or sunshine, for health or food, is just as reasonable as to pray for gifts which the soul only can receive—increased love, joy, peace, long-suffering, gentleness, goodness, faith. All such prayers presuppose the truth that God is not the slave of His own rules of action; that He can innovate upon His work without forfeiting His perfection; that law is only our way of conceiving of His regularized working, and not an external force which governs and moulds what we recognize as His work. It dissolves into thin air, as we look hard at it, this fancied barrier of inexorable law; and as the mist clears off, beyond there is the throne of the Moral King of the universe, in Whose eyes material symmetry is as nothing when compared with the spiritual well-being of His moral creatures.

A second barrier to the efficacy of prayer is sometimes discovered in the truth that all which comes to pass is foredetermined in the predestination of God. How is the efficacy of prayer to be reconciled, asks the fatalistic predestinarian, with the boundless power and knowledge of God?

Is not everything that happens to us the decision of an Almighty, Wise, Beneficent Will; a Will which, in human phrase, has ordained it from all eternity? Could this Will have been, could It be, other than It is? Has time any meaning for It? Is It not in Its Omniscience and Omnipotence eternally what It is? Where, then, is there any room for the effect of prayer? Can it be conceived that the erring understanding and finite will of the creature will be allowed to impose its decisions on the infallible Mind and resistless determinations of God? Surely if we are to go on praying, after recognizing the Sovereignty of God, we must give up the notion of exerting a real influence upon the Divine Will: we must content ourselves with resignation, with bringing our minds into conformity with that which, as a matter of fact, is quite beyond the range of our influence.

This language does but carry us into one department of the old controversy between the defenders of the sovereignty of God on the one side, and the advocates of the free will of man on the other. The very idea of God, as it occurs to the human mind, and the distinct statements of revelation, alike represent the Divine Will as exerting sovereign and resistless sway. If it were otherwise, God would not be Almighty, that is, He would not be God. On the other hand, our daily experience and the language of Scripture both assure us that man is literally a free agent: his freedom is the very ground of his moral and religious responsibility. Are these two truths hopelessly incompatible with each other? So it may seem at first sight; and if we escape the danger of denying the one in the supposed interests of the other, if we shrink from sacrificing God's sovereignty to man's free will with Arminius, and from sacrificing man's freedom to God's sovereignty with Calvin, we can only express a wise ignorance by saying, that to us they seem like parallel lines which must meet at a point in eternity, far beyond our present range of view. We do know, however, that being both true, they cannot really contradict each other; and that in some manner, which we cannot formulate, the Divine Sovereignty must not merely be compatible with, but must even imply the perfect freedom of created wills. So it is with prayer and the Divine predestination. God orders all that happen to us, and, in virtue of His infinite knowledge, by eternal decrees. But He also says to us, in the plainest language, that He does answer prayer, and that practically His dealings with us are governed in matters of the greatest importance as well as of the least by the petitions which we address to Him. What if prayers and actions, to us at the moment perfectly spontaneous, are eternally foreseen and included within the all-embracing Predestination of God, as factors and causes, working out that final result which, beyond all dispute, is the product of His good pleasure? Whether I open my mouth or lift my hand, is, before my doing it, strictly within the jurisdiction and power of my personal will; but however I may decide, my decision, so absolutely free to me, will have been already incorporated by the All-seeing,

All-controlling Being as an integral part, however insignificant, of His one all-embracing purpose, leading on to effects and causes beyond itself. Prayer too is only a foreseen action of man which, together with its results, is embraced in the eternal predestination of God. To us this or that blessing may be strictly contingent on our praying for it; but our prayer is nevertheless so far from necessarily introducing change into the purpose of the Unchangeable, that it has been all along taken, so to speak, into account by Him. If then, with "the Father of Lights" there is in this sense "no variableness, neither shadow of turning," it is not therefore irrational to pray for specific blessings, as we do in the Litany, because God works out His plans not merely in us but by us; and we may dare to say that that which is to us a free self-determination, may be not other than a foreseen element of His work.

A third barrier supposed to interfere with the efficacy of prayer is the false idea of the Divine dignity which is borrowed from our notions of human royalties. It is assumed that a supreme governor cannot be expected to take account of trifling circumstances, or to decide between petty and conflicting claims. He legislates for the universe; but it is not to be supposed that He will also discharge all the minute and harassing duties of a local executive. The power of prayer implies a special providence, and a special providence, we are told, is beneath the dignity of God. We have already encountered this line of thought, not in its practical bearings upon prayer, but as it affects our belief as to the Divine

Nature. " Do you imagine, men ask, when you reflect upon the vast universe in which we live—upon that immeasurable space—upon those innumerable worlds—upon those systems beyond systems of suns which are discovering themselves slowly but surely to our telescopes—that He who made this mighty whole has nothing to do but to listen to the little story of your wants and hopes and fears? He has instituted some good and universal rules of government under which you live: if they sometimes bear hardly upon you, your case is only that of others, and you must take your chance. To expect Him to suspend or to revoke His legislation on your particular account, is to sacrifice common sense to outrageous egotism; the egotism which can suppose that a petty individual life, a worm crawling on the surface of one of His smallest planets, can be an object of this particular consideration and interest to the Almighty Creator."

Even at the risk of representing human egotism, it must be here and again asserted that man's place in the creation is not determined by the considerations which this objection supposes. In the eyes of an intellectual and spiritual being, material bulk is not the only or the highest test of greatness. If God is not to be supposed to be mainly interested in vast accumulations of senseless matter; if there be in the estimate of a Moral Being other and worthier measures of greatness; if the organic be higher than the inorganic; and that which feels than that which has no feeling; if that which thinks be higher than that which only feels; and that which freely conforms to moral will higher than that which only thinks; if a fly be really a nobler thing than a granite mountain, and a little child than a rhinoceros or a mammoth,—then we need not acquiesce in this depreciatory estimate of man's place in creation, or of his claims upon the ear of God. On his bodily side man is insignificant enough. As a spirit conscious of his own existence, and determining his action in the freedom of his will, he does not deceive himself in believing that God has crowned him with an especial glory and honour among the visible creatures.[1] But even if man were not thus honoured, it is, as we have seen, no part of the Divine dignity to be inattentive even to the lowest creatures of His hand. The Throne of heaven is not modelled upon the type of an Oriental despotism, and God's Greatness is not compromised by the duties of administration any more than it is heightened by the enactment of law. The Infinite Mind is not less capable of formulating the most universal principles because He enters with perfect sympathy and intelligence into each of our separate wants and efforts, the wants and efforts of creatures who are really greater, because infinitely more like their Creator, than are the largest stars and suns.

A fourth barrier to the efficacy of prayer is supposed to be discoverable in an inadequate conception of the interests of human beings as a whole. To suppose that God can answer individual prayers for specific blessings is incon-

[1] Ps. viii. 5.

sistent, we are told, with any serious appreciation of human interests. One man or nation asks for that which may be an injury to another. The Spaniards prayed for the success of their Armada: the English prayed against it. Both could not be listened to. The weather cannot consult the convenience of everybody at once: and therefore the specific prayers of well-meaning villagers, if they could be attended to, could only be attended to by a God who, instead of being the Father of all His creatures, reserved special indulgences for His favourites.

Here it is natural to remark that if God should think fit to grant a large proportion of the particular requests which would be found among the daily prayers of an earnest Christian, He would not, to say the least, thereby do any injury to others, whether they were Christians or not. Prayer for the highest well-being of any human being may be granted without damaging other human beings. If God should condescend in answer to prayer to teach one of His servants more humility, purity, or love, this would not oblige Him to withdraw spiritual graces from any others in order to do it. Nor are other persons the worse for coming into contact with one whom God has made loving, or pure, or humble, in answer to prayer. Is it not nearer the truth to say that they are likely to be much better, and therefore that a large number of answers to prayer for personal blessings necessarily extend in their effects beyond those who are immediately blessed?

But observe further that every prayer for specific blessings in a Christian soul is tacitly, if not expressly, conditioned. The three conditions which are always understood are given at the beginning of the Lord's Prayer—"Hallowed be Thy name, Thy kingdom come, Thy will be done." In effect these three conditions are only one. If a change of weather, or a restoration to health or any blessing be prayed for, a Christian petitioner deliberately wills that his prayer should be refused, supposing that to grant it should in any way obscure God's glory in other minds, or hinder the advance of His kingdom, and so contravene what must be His will. Every Christian tacitly adds to every prayer, "Nevertheless not my will but Thine be done." All Christian prayer takes it for granted, first, that the material world exists for the sake of, and is entirely subordinate to, the interests of the moral; and, secondly, that God is the best judge of what the true interests of the moral world really are. Therefore, if his specific petition is not granted, a Christian will not conclude that his real prayer is unanswered. His real prayer was from the first that God's Name might be hallowed among men by the advance of His kingdom and the doing of His Will, through God's granting a particular request which he urges. He knows that his own highest object may be best secured by the refusal of the very blessing for which he pleads; and he puts his finite knowledge and his narrow sympathies into the hands of Infinite Wisdom and Infinite Love, with perfect confidence that the final decision will be the best answer to his real and deepest prayer. It is thus that he realizes the promise, "Every one that asketh receiveth." He too receives that which he really wants, though his specific petition should be refused.

A last barrier to faith in the efficacy of prayer is really to be discovered in man's idea of his own self-sufficiency. It can scarcely be doubted that one of the excellences of our character as a nation is constantly a source of danger to our faith in the power of prayer. Pelagius was himself a native of Britain; and the old heresy of substituting human self-sufficiency for dependence on the grace and help of God is very congenial to the temper which we English cultivate, with such success, in individual action and in political life. After all, we say, do we not depend on our own efforts for being what we are, and for doing what we do? Whatever God may see fit to do for us, our best form of prayer is work; it is the determination to secure what we want by personal efforts to get it. The indolent or the imaginative may be left to lengthen out their litanies; but practical men will fall back upon the wise proverb, that "God helps those who help themselves."

Here, however, it must be insisted on by the one side, and admitted on the other, that many objects of prayer are altogether out of the reach of human effort, and that if they are to be secured at all, they must be given freely by God. But the fact of our moral freedom, as felt in the capacity for work, to which Pelagianism appeals, is not more clear than the fact of our dependence. Do what we will, we depend on others. We are linked to them by a thousand ties; we are, all of us, acted upon most powerfully by the circumstances which surround us; the governing moods of thought and feeling within ourselves are often determined by these circumstances. This is true of "self-made men," as we call them, not less than of others. How much did not Faraday owe to Sir Humphrey Davy! And this dependence upon circumstances is in fact dependence upon things which God controls. Facts are not less facts because they seem to be incompatible; because the effort to reconcile them teaches our reason that its limits are narrower than we wish. It is easier to say that man is entirely free, that he depends on nothing; or to say that man is simply the creature of circumstances, that he is never really free; than to say, what is the real truth, that man is, in his entire freedom, absolutely dependent, that he is, in his entire dependence, absolutely free. Yet this apparent paradox is the literal truth, which refuses to ignore facts in order to make the task of reason easier, and to enable it the better to round off its trenchant but inconclusive theories about human action. And because life is so subtle an intermixture of dependence and action, prayer is the most practical of all forms of work; it is at once the activity of man's freedom, and the expression of his dependence; and the answer which it wins is not less, in one sense, the result of human effort, than in another it is the work of God.

And thus it is in and by prayer that the two governing

elements of religious life, thought and work, alike find their strongest impulse and their point of unity. Such is our weakness, that we constantly tend to a one-sided use of God's gifts. We are either absorbingly speculative and contemplative on the one hand, or we are absorbingly practical and men of action on the other. Either exaggeration is fatal to the true life of religion, which binds the soul to God by faith as well as by love; by love not less than by faith; by a life of energetic service not less truly than by a life of communion with light and truth. It is in prayer that each element is at once quickened in itself, and balanced by the presence of the other. The great masters and teachers of Christian doctrine have always found in prayer their highest source of illumination. Not to go beyond the limits of the English Church, it is recorded of Bishop Andrewes that he spent five hours daily on his knees. The greatest practical resolves that have enriched and beautified human life in Christian times have been arrived at in prayer; ever since the day when, at the most solemn service of the Apostolical Church, the Holy Ghost said, "Separate Me Barnabas and Saul for the work whereunto I have called them."[1] It is prayer which prevents religion from degenerating into mere religious thought on the one side, or into mere philanthropy on the other. In prayer the man of action will never become so absorbed in his work as to be indifferent to the truth, which is its original motive. In prayer the man of

[1] Acts xiii. 2.

study and contemplation will never forget that truth is given, not so much that it may interest and stimulate our understandings, as that it may govern and regenerate our life. And thus it is that prayer is of such vital importance to the well-being of the soul. Study may be dispensed with by those who work with their hands for God: handiwork may be dispensed with by those who seek Him in books and in thought. But prayer is indispensable; alike for workers and students, alike for scholar and peasant, alike for the educated and the unlettered. For we all have to seek God's Face above; we all have souls to be sanctified and saved; we all have sins and passions to beat back and to conquer. And these things are achieved pre-eminently by prayer, which is properly and representatively the action of religion. It is the action whereby we men, in all our frailty and defilement, associate ourselves with our Divine Advocate on high, and realize the sublime bond which in Him, the One Mediator between God and man, unites us in our utter unworthiness to the Strong and All-holy God.

That prayer, sooner or later, is answered, to all who have prayed earnestly and constantly, is, in different degrees, a matter of personal experience. David, Elijah, Hezekiah, Daniel, the Apostles of Christ, were not the victims of an illusion, in virtue of which they connected particular events which would have happened in any case with prayers that preceded it. They who never pray, or who never pray with the humility, confidence, and importunity that wins its way to the Heart of God, cannot speak from experience as to the effects of prayer; nor are they in a position to give credit, with generous simplicity, to those who can. But, at least, on such a subject as this, the voice of the whole company of God's servants may be held to counterbalance a few *à priori* surmises or doctrines; and it is the very heart of humanity itself which from age to age mounts up with the Psalmist to the Eternal Throne—"O Thou That hearest prayer, unto Thee shall all flesh come."[1] And Christians can penetrate within the veil. They know that there is a majestic pleading, which for eighteen centuries has never ceased, and which is itself omnipotent—the pleading of One who makes their cause His own: they rest upon the Divine words, "Whatsoever ye shall ask the Father in My Name, He will give it you."[2]

A time will probably come to most of us, if it has not come to some already, when we shall wish that the hours at our command, during the short day of life, had not been disposed of as they have. After all, this world is a poor thing to live for, when the next is in view. Whatever be their claims, created beings have no business to be sitting on that highest throne within the soul that belongs to the Creator. Yet, for all that, too often they do sit there. And time is passing. Of that priceless gift of time, how much will one day be seen to have been lost; how ruinous shall we deem our investment of this our most precious stock! How many interests, occupations, engagements,

[1] Ps. lxv. 2. [2] S. John xvi. 23.

friendships—I speak not of the avowed ways of "killing time," as it is termed with piteous accuracy—will be then regarded only as so many precautions for building our house upon the sand: as only so many expedients for assuring our failure to compass the true end of our existence! It may not now seem possible that we should ever think thus. Life is like the summer's day; and in the first fresh morning we do not realize the noon-day heat, and at noon we do not think of the shadows lengthening across the plain, and of the setting sun, and of the advancing night. Yet, to each and all, the sunset comes at last; and those who have made most of the day are not unlikely to reflect most bitterly how little they have made of it. Whatever else they may look back upon with thankfulness or with sorrow, it is certain that they will regret no omissions of duty more keenly than neglect of prayer; that they will prize no hours more than those which have been passed, whether in private or in public, before that Throne of Justice and of Grace upon which they hope to gaze throughout eternity.

LECTURE VI.

Palm Sunday.

THE MEDIATOR, THE GUARANTEE OF RELIGIOUS LIFE.

S. Matt. xxiii. 41.

Jesus asked them saying, What think ye of Christ?

AT length, we reach the limits which the season assigns to our scanty treatment of a subject that is in itself inexhaustible. The relationship or bond between God and the soul of man, which we term religion, is obscured and interrupted on man's side by sin; it is reasserted and strengthened by prayer. But no human efforts can of themselves avail to establish or to restore it. If God answers the prayers of individuals, has He answered the prayer of prayers; the great prayer of humanity in all the ages? Has He deigned to grant the prayer that He, too, would on His side give some sign or pledge of real communion with us; that He would not leave us to ourselves, walking after our own ways, feeling after Him if haply we might find Him, but only feeling on, century after century, in the twilight of reason; that He would, in prophetic language, rend the heavens and come down, and bid the skies pour down righteousness? Is religion only a human instinct or effort upon which no encouragement, no sanction, no corresponding and invigorating acknowledgment has been bestowed from on high? Or has God spoken? Has He unveiled Himself? Have the clouds and darkness that are round about Him rolled away, so that the righteousness and judgment which are the habitation of His seat might become clearly manifest to us?

If we really believe God to be a Moral Being, we shall be prepared to find that He has spoken to us. The strength of the confidence with which we anticipate a revelation will vary exactly with our faith in the morality of God. If He were only an intelligence, or a force, there would be no reason or apology for listening to hear whether any voice breaks the silence of the spheres. But if He has, or rather is, a Heart; if the moral qualities which are discoverable in ourselves have any transcendent and majestic counterpart in Him; then, supposing the question whether He has given a revelation to be for us still unanswered, or even unexamined, we do well to traverse all the corridors of history, to take counsel with the current wisdom and experience of the living, and to cross-question the recorded convictions of the dead, until we see reason to hope that a solution is at least at hand; until "the day dawn and the day-star arise in our hearts."

Already, indeed, and almost at each stage of our progress, we have ever and anon halted our steps, and hushed other disputants around us, that we might listen to One Whose place among men, at least as a Master and Teacher of religion, does not really enter into controversy. It is He Who has set forth in its fulness the parental character of God. It is He who has fully unveiled to the eye of the human soul the secret of its boundless capacities, and of its disheartening impotence. It is He Who by His life of unassailable purity, and by His death of voluntary sacrifice, has lighted up the dark realities of moral evil. It is His example, His precepts, it is widespread faith in His assistance and intercession, which have popularized prayer, without degrading its idea. It is through Him that prayer has come to be the most serious and welcome occupation of the noblest and purest in the human family; the continuous expression of a desire to assert and strengthen the link which binds man to the Source and End of his existence. And thus, besides placing before us the idea of religion, He has, as no other, taught us to know Him between Whom and ourselves religion is a bond; and what it is, call we it disease or antagonist, that breaks religion up; and what the spiritual action in which it is especially embodied and re-asserted. Has He done more for religion than this? Is His relation towards it only an external one, such as was that of a Raphael or a Michael Angelo towards their majestic creations, such as was that of a Newton or a Cuvier towards the great subjects of their lifelong study? Or is He, besides being a Master and Teacher of religion, something more, and altogether distinct from this? Is He the masterpiece of His own art? Is He the subject of His own teaching? Does He enter into the object-matter of religion as an integral part of it? Is He not merely the greatest of religious teachers, but also the first and greatest of religious lessons which God has given to man? Is He, in short, God's answer in history to man's constant aspiration heavenward; the impersonated bond between God and man; a "Mediator," as Scripture terms it, Who bridges over the chasm which sin had opened between earth and heaven?

In pausing to consider this question, it is natural to every Christian heart to express the joy of finding ourselves at His blessed feet, Whose name is above every Name that is pronounced, whether in His temples or elsewhere. On the last five Sundays in which you have accompanied me with your generous sympathy, it has often happened to us to stray for a while into schools of thought, where He, our Lord, is either unknown, or denied His due. We have occasionally been listening to teachers and glancing at systems which profess, in whatever sense, to be able to dispense with Him. No men love home as do those whose duty has for awhile obliged them to reside abroad; and the atmosphere of the New Testament and of the Church is not the less welcome, because it is a change from that of human literatures and of earthly philosophies. To-day we cease, at least in the main, to measure the forms and density of the clouds which veil the face of heaven from sad but eager multitudes. We pass into the light and warmth of the Sun of Righteousness, to occupy ourselves from first to last with His glory and His beauty; we advance to recognize, as I trust, in Him the living bond of unity between the great empire of souls on the one hand, and the King Eternal, Immortal, Invisible on the other.

Jesus Christ is a Name around which a vast accumulation of histories, ideas, beliefs, have gathered. Christianity has many aspects; literary, philosophical, moral, historical, political, theological, spiritual, practical. What is the religious aspect of Christianity and of Christ? What is the aspect which exhibits our Lord's relation to religion, considered as the bond between God and the human soul?

I.

"What think ye of Christ?" Is He a subject of the highest historical interest? No educated man, at least, whatever be his faith or his life, can deny the reality or the greatness of Christ's place in human history. Nothing is more certain in the annals of mankind than this, that Jesus Christ lived in Palestine, and was put to death eighteen centuries and a half ago. This fact belongs to general human knowledge, just as much as does the life of Julius Cæsar, or of Alexander the Great, or of Socrates, or of Mahomet. Nobody, indeed, does deny the general fact.

Strauss, for instance, though he endeavours to distinguish between the residuary historical element in the Gospels, and the incrustation of legend, which, in his opinion, has somehow become associated with it, yet fully admits that there is history in the Gospels; he admits that Jesus Christ lived and died in the age of Tiberius. And if even this be admitted, the life and death of Jesus Christ must possess for any intelligent man the highest possible degree of interest. He must feel that, in point of social and historical importance, it stands alone. No doubt, at the time, the Cæsar Tiberius was everywhere on the lips and in the minds of men; while the retired religious Teacher, as He seemed to be, in Palestine, was by His teaching, His acts, and the opposition which they aroused, only furnishing a little conversation and excitement to the peasantry and to the officials of a remote province. But if the importance of a life is to be measured by its results in history and to civilization, even although we should put all religious and even moral considerations aside, who would think most of the Emperor? What is the lasting and living influence which Tiberius now exerts upon the world, except it be to furnish a thesis now and then to clever essay writers, who wish indirectly to attack or to defend modern imperialism? But who can deny that at this moment, explain it how we will, Jesus Christ, His life, His work, His Person, lives in the hearts of multitudes as the object of most cherished and devoted homage; that He governs the ideas, the aspirations, the social and political action of millions of mankind; that the most active and enterprising section of the human family, still, in various senses, places itself under the shadow of His Name and patronage; and that if He has many opponents, there is no serious probability of His being spiritually or intellectually dethroned? All this is a matter of simple observation. The truth of it is most obvious to those who know most about human affairs and human history. And it at once invests the earthly Life of Christ, and all that illustrates and belongs to it, with the highest practical and speculative interest; with the interest which belongs to the great problems of past history, and with the interest which belongs to those great living forces that make themselves felt day by day around us, and contribute powerfully towards determining the current of events.

Not to be interested in the life of Jesus Christ, then, is to be, I do not say irreligious, but unintelligent. It is to be insensible to the nature and claims of the most powerful force that has ever moulded the thought and swayed the destinies of civilized man. But to feel this interest, it is almost unnecessary to add, a man need not even profess to be a Christian. He may indeed be earnestly opposed to Christianity: and his opposition can scarcely in any case be formidable, unless he has given his mind to the careful study of that which he opposes. To such men as Celsus, or Lucian, or Porphyry, or the apostate Emperor Julian, or the philosopher of Ferney, Christianity was a matter of the deepest intellectual interest. Men do not write like Celsus, or act like Julian, or epigrammatize with the bitterness of Voltaire, about a doctrine in which they feel little concerned. Nay, in order to have such an interest, a man need not be an active opponent of Christianity. Looking upon it with the eye, and only with the eye, of a philosopher; jealously excluding from his estimate every trace of passion, whether it be the passion of hatred or the passion of affection; he may yet understand that it is too great, too powerful, in a word, too original a phenomenon, to be ignored, or rather not to be investigated with patient perseverance. Such might seem to have been the case with that most accomplished of modern critics, the late M. Saint-Beuve. His History of Port-Royal betrays an intimate acquaintance with the most delicate and beautiful forms of Christian faith and Christian love. None knew better than he the claims of Jesus Christ—of His life in itself, and of His place in history—upon the attention of all earnest students of nature and of man. No pages are more marked than his by a sustained and rigid justice which is incapable of condescending to a phrase that is dictated by any but that which the writer intends and believes to be a severely critical judgment. This lofty impartiality could not but make him write at times like a devoted Christian in virtue of his moral and literary sympathies; and many men have read him without suspecting his real place in the world of thought. Yet, at his last hours, we are told, he purposely declined the ordinary consolations of a Christian deathbed: his interest in Christianity did not imply a bond to any living person with Whom, in the most solemn and critical moments of existence, there are histories to be reviewed, and accounts to be settled.

That a literary and historical interest in Christianity and Christ has its value, who would deny? It may, in union with faith and love, achieve services of no common order for the kingdom of the truth. It may, under any circumstances, enable Christians to realize the historical settings of their faith, more truly and vividly than would otherwise be possible. Thus, in a very creditable sense, it may hew wood and draw water for the sacred camp, and we must thank it with all our hearts for its services. But it is not of itself a religious interest. It is only an intellectual and scholarly taste dealing with a religious subject-matter. It is one thing to cleanse the glasses of a powerful telescope; it is another to use them as they should be used by an observer and student of the heavens.

II.

But the question must occur, What was it in Jesus Christ which gave Him, in spite of social and political insignificance, so commanding, so unrivalled a position in history? The least answer that can be given—I am far from implying that it is an adequate answer—is, that His character made a profound, an ineffaceable impression upon

His contemporaries; an impression so deep and abiding, that it moved them, peasants and paupers as they were, to achieve the moral revolution of the civilized world. And we are told that admiration for Christ's human character is still the sustaining element in Christianity; that it explains its perpetuation as it explains its original victories; that it furnishes, in fact, the true answer to the question, "What think ye of Christ?" Undoubtedly the appreciation of moral character is a higher and more religious thing than the appreciation of any external historical fact, however imposing. In order to enter into the political consequences of a decisive campaign, a man requires only a well-stored and cultivated intellect; in order to do justice to a saintly character the observer must have that which is infinitely higher in itself, though of less account among men—a sensitive moral instinct, a tender and penetrating heart. And yet, happily, the higher gift is the more common. The questions which may be raised about our Lord's genealogies in the first and third Evangelists can only be answered by a few well-trained scholars. But every child can feel the pathos of the relief suddenly given to the hungry multitudes; of the visit to the house of mourning at Bethany; of the successive incidents of the stern conflict with the Jews of Jerusalem; of the Last Supper; of the Agony; of the Betrayal; of the Cross. A great character, even more than a great picture, or a great poem, or a magnificent mountain, speaks for itself. It commends itself to average men, even though they cannot take their sympathies to pieces, and say precisely what is the feature in it that fascinates them. There is that in their humanity which responds, however imperfectly, to the form of moral beauty before them, and they surrender themselves to an instinct which they do not explain, but which they can implicitly trust.

Thus it is that our Lord's simplicity, His self-sacrifice, His love of the humble and of the poor, joined to His resistless moral ascendancy, His fearless courage, His strength which is so entirely compatible with the utmost tenderness, touches us all. Nothing perhaps shews Jesus Christ more clearly to us than the circumstances under which He delivered the Sermon on the Mount. For here we are convinced that His character was so far from being a product whether of His nation or of His age, as to be in marked opposition to some of their ruling tendencies. In the Jew of the age of Tiberius, the national feeling, intensified by the Roman conquest, had almost killed out the human. The children of the men who under David and Solomon had ruled Western Asia, beheld on every side the symbols of their political slavery. The Roman legionaries were keeping guard near the temple; the Roman tax-gatherer was making his presence felt in every home. And so the Jew wrapped himself more and more closely and sullenly in devotion to the ideas and institutions of his ancestors, and looked forward to a time when the prophecies would be fulfilled in the rigid political sense in which he read them; when the Roman invader would be driven by an indignant people, headed by their King Messiah, from the sacred soil. There were adventurers in that age who really endeavoured to meet this predominating national temper, and the effort led to some well-known catastrophes. And doubtless it was such a political expectation as this which was kindled in the breast of multitudes by the announcement throughout Galilee that the Kingdom of Heaven was at hand. The phrase fired their imaginations. They followed the Teacher Who uttered it out of their towns and villages to a distant hill-side, that they might listen, as they trusted, to His plan for an approaching insurrection or for a decisive campaign. And what was His manifesto? He uttered the Beatitudes; He compared the Pharisaic with the true morality; He proclaimed the law and unfolded the prospects of a spiritual empire, of the kingdom of the truth.

It is not in the unrivalled exhibition of any one form of human excellence, whether purity or humility, or charity, or courage, or veracity, or self-denial, or justice, or consideration for others, that we best appreciate the significance of our Lord's human character. It is in the equal balance of all excellence, in the absence of any warping, disturbing, exaggerating influence, that modern writers have been forward to recognize a moral sublimity, which they can discover nowhere else in history. The subject has been handled by a distinguished living layman, who certainly cannot be supposed to have approached it with any strong ecclesiastical bias. He observes that "there are many peculiarities arising out of personal and historical circumstances, which are incident to the best human characters, and which would prevent any one of them from being universal or final as a type. But the type set up in the Gospels as the Christian type seems to have escaped all these peculiarities, and to stand out in unapproached purity, as well as in unapproached perfection of moral excellence." [1] Accordingly he argues that it can be said to belong exclusively to neither of the "two hemispheres in the actual world of moral excellence—the noble and the amiable, or, in the language of moral taste, the grand and the beautiful." It belongs to both of them, "perfectly and undistinguishably, the fusion of the two classes of qualities being complete, so that the mental eye, though it be strained to aching, cannot discern whether that on which it gazes be more the object of reverence or of love." [2] This type is equally free from sexual peculiarities; it combines the strength of manhood with feminine tenderness so completely as to leave no room for a supplementary female type that should complete the ideal of Christian humanity. [3] It sets before us an image of pure beneficence, disengaged from all peculiar social circumstances which would disqualify a character from being universal and the ideal, yet adapted to all. [4] If that type of character was constructed by human intellect, we must at least bear in mind that "it was constructed at the confluence of three races, the

[1] On some supposed Consequences of the Doctrine of Historical Progress: A Lecture. By Goldwin Smith, M.A. 1861.—P. 15.

[2] *Ibid.* p. 16. [3] *Ibid.* p. 17. [4] *Ibid.*

Jewish, the Greek, and the Roman, each of which had strong national peculiarities of its own. A single touch, a single taint of any one of those peculiarities, and the character would have been national, not universal; transient, not eternal. It might have been the highest character in history, but it would have been disqualified for being the ideal." Supposing it to have been "human, whether it were the effort of a real man to attain moral excellence, or a moral imagination of the writers of the Gospels, the chances, surely," he urges, "were infinite against its escaping any tincture of the fanaticism, formalism, and exclusiveness of the Jew—of the political pride of the Roman—of the intellectual pride of the Greek. Yet it escaped them all." [1]

In like manner, the character before us in the Gospels cannot possibly be regarded as a reaction from something else: it is not an antinominian protest against Pharisaism; it is not a fanatical patriotism protesting against servility to the Roman rule; it is not an exaggerated cosmopolitanism in revolt against the narrow patriotism of the Jew: it is the highest self-denial, without having the character of a formalized asceticism; it is, in short, "the essence of man's moral nature, clothed with a personality so vivid and intense as to excite, through all ages, the most intense affection; yet divested of all those peculiar characteristics, the accidents of place and time, by which human personalities are marked." "What other notion than this," asks

[1] *Ibid.* p. 18.

the writer, "can philosophy form of Divinity manifest on earth?"[1]

These eloquent and sincere words of Professor Goldwin Smith will need no recommendation or comment. And yet they suggest a question, which is in the path of our subject, and which, under any circumstances, cannot be overlooked. This ideal Character of the Gospels is, on one side, at issue with what we should abstractedly conceive to be a perfect *human* ideal. For He who presents it to us proclaims Himself, in terms and to an extent which are altogether inconsistent with any true ideal of a purely creaturely perfection. In the words of another writer of our day, "The unbounded personal pretensions which Christ advances, remain throughout a subject of ever-recurring astonishment. It is common, in human history, to meet with those who claim some superiority over their fellows. Men assert a pre-eminence over their fellow-citizens or fellow-countrymen, and become rulers of those who were at first their equals; but they dream of nothing greater than of some partial control over the actions of others for the short space of a lifetime. Few, indeed, are there to whom it is given to influence future ages. Yet some men have appeared who have been as levers to uplift the earth and roll it in another course. Homer, by creating literature; Socrates, by creating science; Cæsar, by carrying civilization inward from the shores of the Mediterranean; Newton, by starting science upon a career of steady progress,—may be said to have attained this eminence. But

[1] *Ibid.* p. 22.

these men gave a single impact, like that which is conceived to have first set the planets in motion: Christ claims to be a perpetual attractive power, like the sun, which determines their orbit. They contributed to men some discovery, and passed away: Christ's discovery is Himself. To humanity, struggling with its passions and its destiny, He says—'Cling to Me: cling ever closer to Me.' . . . He represented himself as the Light of the world, as the Shepherd of the souls of men, as the Way to immortality, as the Vine or Life-Tree of humanity. . . . He commanded men to leave everything and attach themselves to Him; . . . He declared Himself King, Master, and Judge of men; . . . He promised to give rest to all the weary and heavy-laden; . . . He instructed His followers to hope for life from feeding on His body and His blood." [1]

If this statement only suggests the complete truth, it is true as far as it goes. It might be sustained by a hundred texts. That which is so striking, so overpowering in the Gospels, is perhaps less the precise language which our Lord uses about Himself, than the consistent bearing which He assumes towards His disciples and mankind. His attitude is that of One Who takes His claims for granted; Who has no errors to confess, no demands to explain, or to apologize for; no restraining instinct of self-distrust to keep Him in the background; no shrinking from high command, based upon a sense of the possible superiority

[1] "Ecce Homo," pp. 176–177.

of those around Him. It is the bearing of One Who claims to be the First of all, the Centre of all, with entire simplicity indeed, but also with unhesitating decision.

Let us dwell more in detail upon some of the language which Jesus Christ really uses about Himself. He is greater than the most venerable names in Jewish antiquity; greater than the men whose greatness had been felt most widely and deeply beyond the boundaries of Israel. He is greater than Jonah, whose preaching brought Nineveh to penitence;[1] greater than Solomon, in whom not Israel only, but the whole East, recognized the wisest of men.[2] Not merely is He David's descendant; He is David's Lord.[3] When Abraham was yet unborn, He was already in existence.[4] Thus He could refer to "the glory which He had with the Father before the world was,"[5] and to the fall of the rebel-spirit, which he had witnessed.[6] God is, in an entirely unique sense, His Father;[7] the Jews feel that He uses the word in a manner which implies a tremendous claim.[8] For, indeed, He is conscious of being "from above,"[9] of having "come down from heaven,"[10] of having come forth from being

[1] S. Matt. xii. 41. [2] S. Matt. xii. 42.

[3] S. Matt. xxii. 41-46; Ps. cx. 1.

[4] S. John viii. 56, 57, 58; cf. i. 15, 27, 30.

[5] S. John xvii. 5; cf. verse 24. [6] S. Luke x. 18.

[7] S. Matt. x. 32; xv. 13; xvi. 17; xviii. 19; xxvi. 39, 42; S. Luke xxiii. 46; xxiv. 49; S. John v. 30; x. 29; xiv. 2, 6.

[8] S. John v. 17-18, πατέρα ἴδιον ἔλεγε τὸν Θεὸν, ἴσον ἑαυτὸν ποιῶν τῷ Θεῷ.

[9] S. John viii. 23, ἐγὼ ἐκ τῶν ἄνω εἰμί.

[10] *Ibid.* vi. 38, καταβέβηκα ἐκ τοῦ οὐρανοῦ; v. 51. ὁ ἐκ τοῦ οὐρανοῦ καταβάς.

with the Father,[1] of having come forth out of God.[2] He knows, not merely that He lives; but that He has in Himself, that He is, the Life; Life in the deepest sense of the term,—perfect, blessed, absolute existence; eternally received from the Father, yet shared with Him thus from everlasting to everlasting.[3] Although, then, He is visibly upon the earth, He is still really in Heaven.[4] He is united to the Father not merely by a moral, but by a natural union,[5] and so intimately, that "to have seen Him is to have seen the Father,[6] to have known Him is to have known the Father."[7] He is in the Father, and the Father is in Him, by a perfect reciprocity.[8] Of the Father He only has adequate knowledge: He Himself is known only by the Father.[9] As a consequence, He has all things in common with the Father.[10] Men, whom He wills to redeem, are already His own.[11] The Kingdom of God is His Kingdom.[12] The Angels are His Angels.[13] The "Church of the Living God"[14] is His Church.[15] Power is

[1] *Ibid.* xvi. 28, ἐξῆλθον παρὰ τοῦ πατρὸς, καὶ ἐλήλυθα εἰς τὸν κόσμον.

[2] *Ibid.* viii. 42, ἐκ τοῦ Θεοῦ ἐξῆλθον καὶ ἥκω. Cf. S. John xvii. 8; xvi. 30; Ps. ii. 7; Micah v. 2.

[3] S. John v. 26; xi. 25; xiv. 6; cf. S. John i. 4; 1 S. John i. 1, 2; v. 20.

[4] S. John iii. 13, ὁ υἱὸς τοῦ ἀνθρώπου ὁ ὢν ἐν τῷ οὐρανῷ.

[5] S. John x. 28-30, ἐγὼ καὶ ὁ πατὴρ ἕν ἐσμεν.

[6] *Ibid.* xiv. 9.

[7] *Ibid.* viii. 19.

[8] S. John xiv. 10; xvii. 21, 22.

[9] S. Matt. xi. 27. Cf. S. John vi. 46, ὁ ὢν παρὰ τοῦ Θεοῦ, οὗτος ἑώρακε τὸν πατέρα. *Ibid.* x. 14, 15.

[10] S. John xvi. 15; xvii. 10; cf. S. Matt. xi. 27; Heb. i. 3; S. Matt. xxi. 38; Acts x. 36.; S. John i. 11.

[11] S. John x. 14, 15, 27, 28; xvii. 10-12.

[12] S. Matt. xiii. 41; S. John xviii. 36. Cf. S. Luke i. 33; Rev. xi. 15.

[13] S. Matt. xiii. 41; xvi. 27; xxiv. 31.

[14] 1 Tim. iii. 15.

[15] S. Matt. xvi. 18; cf. Rom. xvi. 16.

given Him not merely over the human race,[1] but also without any assigned limits in heaven and in earth;[2] and the glory with which He will appear at the last day is not other than His Father's.[3] His working in the sphere of sense and time corresponds to the ceaseless activity of the Father.[4] He too quickens and will raise the dead.[5] He too forgives sins, as to the Paralytic;[6] He too will save the world;[7] He will seek and save the lost;[8] He will give eternal life.[9] To Him all judgment is committed, and all nations shall one day be gathered before His Throne.[10] Even now all men are to honour Him, even as they honour the Father.[11]

His words are familiar to our ears; but do we dwell upon their real and awful meaning? What should we think of a religious teacher now who could permit himself to say that Eternal Life consisted in the knowledge of himself as well as in knowledge of the Father;[12] that dislike of himself implied dislike of the Father;[13] that belief in himself secured eternal life;[14] that disbelief in himself involved present condemnation?[15] What, if he should tell us that without him we could do nothing;[16] that united with him, we should bring forth much fruit;[17]

[1] S. John xvii. 2. [2] S. Matt. xxviii. 18. [3] S. Matt. xvi. 27.
[4] S. John v. 17, 19, 20. [5] *Ibid.* verses 21, 28, 29; xi. 25, 40.
[6] S. Matt. ix. 2-7; S. Luke vii. 36-50. [7] S. John iii. 17.
[8] S. Luke xix. 10; ix. 56. [9] S. John xvii. 2.
[10] S. John v. 22, 27; S. Matt. xxv. 31-39. Cf. Is. xi. 3.
[11] S. John v. 20-23. [12] S. John xvii. 3; xii. 44.
[13] S. John xv. 23; S. Luke x. 16. [14] S. John iii. 16; v. 40; vi. 47.
[15] S. John iii. 18; viii. 24. [16] S. John xv. 5; xiv. 6.
[17] S. John xv. 4.

that, although leaving this world before us, he was going to prepare places for us in the Eternal Home;[1] that his name would have resistless power with the Father;[2] that in his name his pupils would cast out devils;[3] that he would send the Divine Spirit from the Father[4] Who, when He came, would glorify the sender?[5] What should we say of the promise of a perpetual presence,[6] of the pretension to found an imperishable society,[7] of the delegation of power to forgive sins,[8] of the claim to be so faultless that in him the Prince of evil had no part whatever?[9]

Much else to the same purpose might be quoted from the three earlier Gospels, as well as from the last; and the question arises, how we are to account for this earnest self-assertion on the part of Jesus Christ, to explain such language? How are we to adjust it, on the one hand, with the sobriety and truthfulness of a perfect human character; on the other, with a due recognition of the rights of God?

There are men who decline to entertain this inquiry. They are not by any means forgetful of God. He weighs upon their conscience, upon their imagination, upon their life of daily thought and action, as the greatest and most solemn of all facts. They are not insensible to the moral beauties of the earthly life of Jesus Christ; on the contrary, they profess to be so enamoured of these beauties, or of

[1] S. John xiv. 2, 3. [2] *Ibid.* xvi. 23; xiv. 13, 14.
[3] S. Mark xvi. 17, 18; cf. 20. [4] S. John xvi. 7.
[5] S. John xvi. 14. [6] S. Matt. xxviii. 20. [7] S. Matt. xvi. 18.
[8] S. John xx. 21-23; S. Matt. xvi. 19; xviii. 18.
[9] S. John xiv. 30.

some of them, as to be impatient of all other aspects of our Lord's Work and Teaching, But they do not allow themselves to reflect steadily upon the question whether their loyalty to the supreme rights of God, and their love for Jesus Christ, do not alike oblige them to "consider the relation which exists between Christ and God." Christian theology appears to them in the light of a wanton importation of worthless metaphysics into the heart of a moral history of simple and faultless beauty; but they do not reflect that their moral ideal itself must fall to pieces, unless they are prepared in some way to attempt the chief problem with which Christian theology deals.

Is our Lord's language imposture? The suggestion can only be mentioned to be condemned by the entire drift and atmosphere of His Life. Is it the hallucination of an enthusiast, so entranced in his idea as to be insensible to the world of facts around him? But even Channing has pointed out that the enthusiasm takes a turn which would be inconceivable, for a deranged enthusiasm, under the circumstances of Jesus Christ: "I can conceive," he says, "of His seating Himself, in fancy, on the throne of David, and secretly pondering the means of His appointed triumphs; but that a Jew should fancy himself the Messiah, and at the same time should strip that character of all the attributes that fired his youthful imagination and heart; that he should start aside from all the feelings and hopes of His age, and should acquire a consciousness of being destined to a wholly new career, and one as unbounded as it was new—

this is exceedingly improbable."[1] Was it, then, only the natural manner of an oriental mind; the habit of seizing truth intuitively and enunciating it authoritatively, in contrast with our western methods of demonstration and argument? But this explanation, even if on other accounts it could be admitted, does not cover the ground required. It does not justify the actual substance and contents of our Lord's language about Himself. It does not explain the fact that His language about Himself is unlike anything which we find in the Hebrew prophets. The prophets, if you will, announce truth in the intuitive manner; but they do not make themselves the subjects and centres of the truth which they announce. They draw the deepest distinctions between themselves and their Master: they are sinners, and He is the All-holy; they are foolish and incapable, He is All-powerful and All-wise. The relation in which Christ claims to stand, both towards the Father and towards mankind, is utterly unanticipated by anything that can be traced in the prophetic literature of Israel; it reveals a Personality distinct in kind from any that had previously appeared in Hebrew history.

And at this point we cannot but observe that our Lord's language about Himself is entirely in harmony with the character of certain of the miracles ascribed to Him in the Gospels. The miraculous element cannot be weeded out of the Gospel narratives, without altogether impugning the historical value of those documents; and to do this mainly

[1] Channing: Works, ii. 56.

because one department or one age of human experience does not positively correspond with what we know as yet about another, is not reasonable. Now, the Gospel miracles fall, speaking roughly, into two classes; they are acts of mercy, or acts of power. In one sense, they are all acts of power; but the motive of compassion towards human suffering apparently predominates in the one class; while, in the other, the reason for working them must be chiefly looked for in the need of demonstrating the personal power of the Agent. Thus, among the miracles of mercy, there are seventeen cases on record of His healing bodily disease; there are six cases of the cure of demoniacal possession, each of which is described in detail; there are three cases of restoration to life. On the other hand, the miracles at Cana in Galilee, and of feeding the four and the five thousand, suggest, first of all, the creative power of the Worker, although it was wielded with a philanthropic object. The element of power is more distinctly and exclusively apparent in His stilling the tempest, and walking on the sea; in His rendering Himself invisible to a hostile multitude; in His awing by a glance the traders in the temple, and the multitude that came to take Him; in His cursing the barren fig-tree. Some of this class of miracles are, in fact, objected to by a recent writer,[1] on the specific ground that they only befit a superhuman personality. We therefore do not strain the import of such miracles in saying that they are, at least, in harmony with Christ's language about His claims and His superhuman Person.

[1] Schenkel: Characterbild Jesu. Absch. iv., Kap. 11, p. 123.

But our Lord's references to Himself are also in keeping with another phenomenon. He was sinless. Upon the positive side of Christ's character we have already dwelt; upon the balanced perfection, the ideal universality of the type. It was a life such as Paganism had not conceived; it was higher than, and distinct from, the unimpeachable justice, the calm superiority to misfortune, the proud self-respect, which constituted, in various proportions, the Pagan ideal. It was a life of love and humility, of the highest forms of holiness, expressed by example as well as recommended by precept. But the most startling moral feature in this life is that we can trace nowhere in it any—the faintest—consciousness of guilt. The best men ordinarily feel the taint of moral evil most constantly and acutely: their language about their sins and shortcomings seems even exaggerated to those who live at a greater distance from the Source of sanctity than they themselves. But Jesus challenges His enemies to convince Him of sin, if they can. He never hints that He has done or said any one thing which needs forgiveness. He teaches His disciples to pray, "Forgive us our trespasses:" He never prays for pardon Himself. Sorrow makes all of us think of that in our past lives, which, as conscience whispers, has but too well deserved it: Jesus, in His sorrow, thinks only of the sins of others. Certainly He is tempted; but there is nothing within Him that can respond to the temptation: He is "holy, harmless, undefiled, separate from sinners." And no attempts to fasten sin upon Him have had a trace of success, except so far as they have gone hand in hand with a denial of His personal claims. Strauss, for example, thinks it not merely fanaticism, but "unjustifiable self-exaltation, for a man to imagine himself so separated from other men, as to set himself before them as their future judge."[1] Strauss, we must admit, is perfectly right, if the claim of Christ to judge the world is not strictly based upon fact. It is strictly impossible to maintain our faith in the faultlessness of His character if we deny that a fundamental necessity of His Being forced Him to draw attention so persistently, so imperiously, to Himself. But, on the other hand, if His words about Himself are sober truth, they only afford another illustration of His compassionate love for those whom He came to enlighten and to save.

Doubtless it has been a favourite object with a modern school, as men have said, "to bring down Jesus from the clouds, and to restore Him, by criticism, to the domain of history." This enterprise assumes that "the theological and metaphysical Christ of the creeds," is a very different person from "the living Christ of the Gospels." But when such criticism enters upon its task, what happens? If, instead of declaiming vaguely against dogma, men really wish to get to the bottom of this problem, they will find that, of two things, one becomes absolutely necessary. Either they must consent to forfeit the moral ideal which they admire in the Gospels, and which, to do them justice, they

[1] Leben Jesu für das Deutsche Volk, p. 242.

are sincerely anxious to preserve; or they must fall back upon those very statements of the creeds which, by affirming Christ's personal Divinity, really and only justify His constant references to Himself, and His unbounded claims upon mankind. His precepts about humility are contradicted by His example, unless His statements about Himself are dictated by that true humility which would rather incur the suspicion of pride than conceal the simple fact. His enforcement of sincerity ceases to awe us, if, in His language about Himself, He was indeed guilty of consistent and almost boundless exaggeration. His very charity loses its lustre, and becomes suspected, if we are forced to feel that He is ever capable of putting Himself unduly forward; its highest forms cease to represent in our eyes the Universal Love; they remind us rather of the efforts of this or that tribune of the people, who clothes a personal ambition beneath the activities of an ostentatious disinterestedness, and whose efforts are at last crowned by a catastrophe which they have really deserved.

If, on the other hand, we bow before the general impression produced by Christ's character, and He be taken at His word, He must be believed to be, in the absolute sense, Divine. There is no room for an intermediate being, such as Arianism imagined, who is neither God nor an angel, in a serious theistic creed. And our Lord's words are strictly inconsistent with what would be sober and true in any creature, however exalted. They are not surpassed; they are only unfolded by the later teaching of apostles and of creeds. The Christ of S. Paul's Epistles is really the Christ of the earliest Evangelist; the Christ of S. John is the Christ of S. Paul; the Christ of the Creeds and the great Councils is the Christ of S. John. He Who alone knows the Father, and Whom none but the Father knows,[1] is the Image of the Father,[2] is in the Form of God,[3] is the Effulgence of God's glory and the exact Impress of His Being,[4] is over all God blessed for ever.[5] He, the only Begotten Son, or God, Which is in the bosom of the Father,[6] is of one substance with the Father,[7] as being "God of the substance of the Father, begotten before all worlds."[8] The later statements may be more elaborate; but they are implied, in all their completeness, by the earlier. Just as an anatomist, from his knowledge of the animal frame, can pronounce upon the age and size of a skeleton of which he only possesses the fragment of a single bone; so with our eye upon S. John, and the Nicene confession, we can see statements in S. Mark which can only be maintained when men acknowledge the consubstantiality of the Son with the Father. There are deep harmonies in truth which, from first to last, bind it in its integrity rigidly together. They cannot be set aside or trifled with; for truths which we in our narrowness deem obscure or unimportant, are often vitally necessary to the maintenance of others which we are better capable of appreciating. Our Blessed Lord's Divinity, instead of obscuring His true

[1] S. Matt. xi. 29. [2] Col. i. 15. [3] Phil. ii. 6. [4] Heb. i. 3.
[5] Rom. ix. 5. [6] S. John i. 18. [7] Nic. Creed. [8] Athan. Creed.

Manhood, is the safeguard and justification of its moral perfectness: and we do the most beautiful of moral histories a fatal injustice, if we forget that, in the words of the Creed, its subject "is perfect God and perfect Man, of a reasonable soul and human flesh subsisting; equal to the Father as touching His Godhead, and inferior to the Father as touching His manhood; Who, although He be God and Man, yet is He not two, but one Christ."[1]

This is the full and solemn truth; that Jesus Christ is not merely the Teacher but the substance of Christianity; not merely the author of the faith which Christians profess, but its central object. For Christians the popular phrase, "the religion of Christ," does not mean, as Lessing suggested, only or chiefly the piety which in the days of His flesh He exhibited towards the Father. It means the piety, the submission of thought and heart, the sense of obligation, the voluntary enthusiastic service, of which He, together and equally with the Father, is the rightful and everlasting Object; which, when He was on earth, He claimed as His due; and which has been rendered to Him now for more than eighteen hundred years by the best and noblest of the human race.

[1] Athanasian Creed.

III.

In Jesus Christ, then, we have the guarantee or bond of religion; He is the means of an actual communication between the soul of man and the Eternal God. "There is one Mediator between God and men, the man Christ Jesus."[1] He is the Mediation in virtue of the very terms of His Being: His office of Mediation is based upon the two Natures which are united in His Single Person. On the one hand, as the Eternal Son, He is One with the All-Holy and Infinite God; on the other, as the child of Mary, He shares all the finiteness and weakness of our manhood; He shares everything with it except its sin. Thus He impersonates and maintains, by the very fact of being what He is, a true vital bond between earth and heaven. To us men, He is the last and most complete unveiling of the interest which God takes in the well-being of His moral and reasonable creatures; the Highest Organ of the Divine Mind and Will; the only and certain channel of those "unsearchable riches"[2] which flow down from the Fountain of all goodness upon the beings whom He has made. Before the Majesty of God He is the unique and ideal Representative of our race: He represents us, not as being what we are, but as being what we were meant to be by the Great Author of our existence. And yet, although we are only weak and sinful, we may unite ourselves to Him by faith, and love, and contrition for the

[1] 1 Tim. ii. 5. [2] Eph. iii. 8.

past, and be "accepted in the Beloved."[1] His obedience as Man, reaching its climax in the self-sacrifice of the Cross, becomes ours through His free grace and mercy. His invigorating life, which restores our race to its original strength and beauty, is still communicated to us by His Spirit and His Sacraments; so that all who will, may "put off the old man, which is corrupt according to the deceitful lusts; and be renewed in the spirit of their minds; and put on the new man, which after God is created in righteousness and true holiness."[2] This cannot be done by fallen man for himself, and out of the resources of his warped and impoverished nature. But "what the law could not do, in that it was weak through the flesh, God sending His own Son in the likeness of sinful flesh, and for sin, condemned sin in the flesh; that the righteousness of the law might be fulfilled in us, who walk not after the flesh, but after the Spirit."[3] Being as He is, Divine as well as Human, Jesus is "made unto us Wisdom, and Righteousness, and Sanctification, and Redemption."[4] Thus in union with Him, those religious aspirations, which are part of our natural outfit, find their true exercise, their full satisfaction. As the Light of the world, He is the satisfaction of the intellect. As "Fairer than the children of men," He is the delight of the heart. As "Holy, harmless, undefiled, separate from sinners," He challenges the submission of the will. Intellect, feeling, moral effort, each have their part in Him. He recognizes, He con-

[1] Eph. i. 6. [2] Eph. iv. 22–24. [3] Rom. viii. 3, 4. [4] 1 Cor. i. 30.

secrates them. He leads them upwards, in and through His own Holy Humanity to the All-wise and All-beautiful. The soul finds that in Him "is the well of Life, and that in His Light it will see light."

Does it seem inconceivable that the Eternal Son of God should have, indeed, thus come among us men, to teach and to save us; to make reconciliation between us and the Almighty Father; to bestow on us the priceless gift of a new Nature; and to lead us back, first one and then another, to our true home and peace? Certainly, it may well move our wonder to think of such grace and mercy. The Christian creed, when once it becomes precious to us, takes us altogether out of the daily range of earthly thoughts and interests, lifting us into a better, and brighter, but not more mysterious, or less real, world than this. The Incarnation and Death of the Everlasting Son seem impossible, only because we do not steadily reflect upon the simple but momentous truths which lie at the root of all religion, and which all who are not Materialists or Pantheists generally admit. Is the Incarnation so improbable, think you, if God is indeed a moral Being, if man has an immortal soul, if moral evil is inherently deadly in itself and in its effects? Do we not name "God," "immortality," "sin," without thinking what we mean; as if these tremendous words were the symbols of trivial commonplaces, which implied nothing beyond themselves? And is not this careless treatment of these solemn truths which we profess to own, the reason why many of us do not understand the truths beyond them? If the awfulness and magnificence of God, the reality of eternity, the power and sting of moral evil, were more often subjects of our thought, would our imaginations be so startled, as they often are, by those doctrines of grace which adjust and harmonize what else is so full of perplexity; by the Incarnation of the Blessed Son of God; by His plenary Atonement on the Cross for the sins of men; by His unceasing Intercession for us before the Father; by the sanctifying energy of His Holy Spirit; by the power of His Sacraments, to renew and sustain our life? Surely the earlier truths are just as full of difficulties for the imagination and the reason as the latter. We put them out of sight as being less importunate; but there they are. That the All-foreseeing and Holy God should have created us at all, is at least as startling as that, having created, He should have redeemed us. Or rather, when we reflect upon His morality, upon His justice, upon His love, we must think that His Redemption of the fallen is really less wonderful than His Creation of a race capable of such signal failure; and we must find in our daily experience of life, of the crimes and sufferings, which so largely compose it, more embarrassment and distress for reverent reason than can be furnished by critical speculations upon the explanatory and consoling truth, that "God so loved the world that He gave His only-begotten Son, that whosoever believeth on Him should not perish, but have everlasting life."[1]

[1] S. John iii. 16.

"Whosoever believeth in Him." It is not then, you say, a matter of strict mathematical demonstration. No; it is not a matter of strict mathematical demonstration. If it were, there would be no more room for faith than there is in the process of learning a proposition of Euclid. Not to acquiesce in the conclusion of a proposition of Euclid, is to be intellectually deficient; but to refuse assent to the Christian creed does not necessarily imply intellectual deficiency. Why not? Because for such assent moral dispositions are necessary as well as intellectual capacity. The evidence for Christianity, intellectually viewed, is something short of mathematical; and intentionally so. Christian truth makes a demand upon the will as well as upon the intellect; and the will, to avoid the foreseen consequences of assent, will often prevent the intellect from doing its work, honestly and thoroughly, in investigating the claims of Christ. This is a reason why so much store is set upon faith in St. Paul's Epistles. Faith is a test of the moral drift of our whole being, and not merely of the soundness or acuteness of our understandings. If an act of faith in Jesus Christ implied no more than an act of assent to the conclusion of a demonstrated proposition; if faith were nothing higher and nobler than the forced result of a victorious assault upon the human understanding, conducted by columns and batteries of mathematical evidence; then all that is said about its moral and spiritual worth, about its purifying and elevating power, would be simply unintelligible. The most accomplished mathematician is not necessarily moral; and the most fervent believers, ancient or modern, have not been always Pascals and Newtons.

Our Lord did, indeed, by His miracles, and notably by His resurrection, address Himself to the experience of His contemporaries in enforcing His claims; and by certain portions of His teaching, He appealed no less truly to the operations of their natural reason. But, in order to accept Him as He is, reason and observation must be seconded by the heart and the conscience. There must be a true desire to know all that can be known of the Author of the law of right and wrong within us. There must be a real anxiety to escape from the moral anomalies of life; a recognition, and sense of human goodness; a strong anticipation that He Who is its Source cannot have left us in weakness and darkness to struggle alone. Why this temper is found in one man and not in another, is a question which carries us back into the deepest secrets of our several moral natures; into the varying histories of our loyalty or disloyalty to God's original gift of natural light. But upon the existence or non-existence of such moral dispositions depends our way of looking at the evidence which Jesus Christ has thought good to set before us on behalf of His claims. In one case that evidence will appear sufficient; insufficient in another. It will be held insufficient by the man who thinks to become a believing Christian, as he would become a mathematician, without any reference to the temper of his heart, or even in spite of its decided bent against the moral teaching of the Gospel. It will be deemed sufficient—nay, more than sufficient—for those who amid perplexities are "waiting for the consolation of Israel."[1] They understand that religious truth, to be embraced at all to any purpose, must be embraced, not simply by a dry assent of the logical understanding, but by a vital act of the whole inward man; by moral sympathies even more earnestly than by an intellectual grasp. Christ, our Lord, in various ways, teaches us as much as this; and Christian apologists can only make that portion of the act of faith which belongs to the understanding easier to it, by removing obstacles to the reception of truth or by exhibiting its inward harmonies. They cannot, if they would, do the work of the Divine Spirit, and control the fevers, the prejudices, the cowardice, the rashness of the heart. He only Who made the heart can soften, or subdue, or change it. He only Who made the light to shine out of darkness can so shine in the hearts of men, as to "give the light of the knowledge of the glory of God in the face of Jesus Christ."[2]

And they to whom He has taught this great lesson will know and feel, that believing in the Divinity of our Incarnate Lord, we stand, as it were, upon the heights of Pisgah; and that a new and vast prospect, grateful to eyes that are wearied with the long glare of the desert, is opening before us. Before us is a land of vineyards and oliveyards; a land flowing with milk and honey. It is a region of repose

[1] S. Luke ii. 25. [2] 2 Cor. iv. 6.

for faith and love; it is an atmosphere where communion with God is easy and natural. It is the proper home of spirituality and benevolence, of that internal and external practice of religion, day by day, which is so altogether higher and better a thing than the profoundest study of its theory. For the Divinity of the Son of God is the adequate warrant of all His promises; of the power of His death; of the gift of His Spirit; of the efficacy of His sacraments; of the converting and hallowing power of His written word; of the Divine character of that society of souls which, by His Spirit, He has organized into His Church since the Day of Pentecost. How vast in their range, how interesting in their idea and scope, how energetically practical in their bearings on all earnest life, are these great Christian doctrines which form the hills and vales of our Gospel Land of Promise! We strain our eyes; we would fain go forward to study their beauties, to try, if it might be, to understand and to surmount their difficulties. But it cannot be;—at least now. If only we sincerely cling by faith and love to our Divine and Human Lord, all else will follow. For the present, like the Magdalen, we can but hold Him by the feet, and entreat Him to teach us that personal devotedness to Himself, which is the secret and soul of genuine religion; since without it the love of God soon dies away into an attenuated mysticism, while the love of man is eventually hollowed out into a mechanical philanthropy. Thinking of Him, praying to Him, working for Him day by day, as our living, tender, mighty, and wise Friend, we strengthen our hold upon the one certain bond between earth and heaven; upon Him through Whom, in all our feebleness and sin, we have real access in one Spirit unto the Father.[1]

Personal devotion to Jesus Christ is the exercise of thought, and of affection, steadily directed upon His adorable Person. But it is also the exercise of will: it is preeminently practical. There is much to be abstained from for His sake; there is much to be done and to be endured; there is some danger, perhaps, of our doing nothing very definite, where the opportunities of action are so various and so complex. And, therefore, that you may do something for Jesus Christ now and here, you are asked to support with your alms the St. James' Penitentiary. Its object is to carry out our Lord's work in the world as the Healer of souls, whom sin has separated from God, by bringing them back to purity and peace through a recovered union with Himself. It has been said that Penitentiaries are too costly a method of restoration from sin. They who speak thus can have thought little to any purpose about either the malignity of moral evil, or the meaning of the Self-sacrifice of the Son of God. The institution which I have named has done and is doing good, and, as we trust, lasting work among our unhappy sisters, who may well be so much less guilty in the eyes of the

[1] Eph. ii. 18.

Eternal Justice than are many upon whom, in this present world, and often to their own endless loss, the breath of censure never falls. Be our case what it may, we surely do well to support an undertaking which honours our Lord, by its disinterested work of unwearied compassion; and which, while labouring for the social recovery of our poor countrywomen, aims much more directly at promoting the eternal well-being of their souls,—as capable as our own of enjoying, through the Divine Mediator, the present and future blessings of religion.

BY THE SAME AUTHOR

I.

The Divinity of our Lord and Saviour *Jesus Christ:* Eight Lectures preached before the University of Oxford, in the Year 1866, on the Foundation of the late Rev. JOHN BAMPTON, M.A., Canon of Salisbury. Fifth Edition. Crown 8vo, 5*s*.

II.

Sermons Preached before the University of *Oxford.* Fourth Edition. Crown 8vo, 5*s*.

III.

A Manual for the Sick; with other Devotions. By Lancelot Andrewes, D.D., sometime Lord Bishop of Winchester. Edited, with a Preface, by H. P. Liddon, M.A. Second Edition. Large Type, with Portrait. 24mo, 2*s*. 6*d*.

IV.

Walter Kerr Hamilton, Bishop of Salisbury. A Sketch, reprinted from "*The Guardian*," with Additions and Corrections. Second Edition. 8vo., limp cloth, 2*s*. 6*d*. ; or, with the Sermon "LIFE IN DEATH," 3*s*. 6*d*.

RIVINGTONS
London, Oxford, and Cambridge

NEW BOOKS

IN COURSE OF PUBLICATION BY

MESSRS. RIVINGTON

WATERLOO PLACE, LONDON

HIGH STREET, OXFORD; TRINITY STREET, CAMBRIDGE

June, 1872

THE BOOK OF CHURCH LAW. *Being an Exposition of the Legal Rights and Duties of the Clergy and Laity of the Church of England. By the* Rev. JOHN HENRY BLUNT, M.A., F.S.A. *Revised by* WALTER F. G. PHILLIMORE, B.C.L., *Barrister-at-Law, and Chancellor of the Diocese of Lincoln.*

Crown 8vo. 7*s.* 6*d.*

HENRI PERREYVE. *By* A. GRATRY, *Prêtre de l'Oratoire, Professeur de Morale Evangélique à la Sorbonne, et Membre de l'Académie Française. Translated, by special permission, by the Author of "A Dominican Artist," "Life of S. Francis de Sales," &c., &c.*

With Portrait. Crown 8vo. 7*s.* 6*d.*

NOTITIA EUCHARISTICA. *A Commentary, Explanatory, Doctrinal, and Historical, on the Order of the Administration of the Lord's Supper, or Holy Communion, according to the use of the Church of England. By* W. E. SCUDAMORE, M.A., *Rector of Ditchingham, and formerly Fellow of St. John's College, Cambridge.*

8vo. 28*s.*

New Publications.

THE HOLY CATHOLIC CHURCH: ITS DIVINE IDEAL, MINISTRY, AND INSTITUTIONS. *A Short Treatise. With a Catechism on each Chapter, forming a Course of Methodical Instruction on the subject. By* EDWARD MEYRICK GOULBURN, D.D., *Dean of Norwich.*

Crown 8vo. [*Nearly Ready.*

A HANDY BOOK ON THE ECCLESIASTICAL DILAPIDATIONS ACT, 1871. *With Remarks on the Qualification and Practice of Diocesan Surveyors. By* EDWARD G. BRUTON, *Fellow of the Royal Institute of British Architects, and Diocesan Surveyor, Oxford.*

Crown 8vo. 3*s.* 6*d.*

SERMONS ON CERTAIN OF THE LESS PROMINENT FACTS AND REFERENCES IN SACRED STORY. *By* HENRY MELVILL, B.D., *late Canon of St. Paul's, and Chaplain in Ordinary to the Queen.*

New Edition. Two vols. Crown 8vo. 5*s.* each.

SOME ELEMENTS OF RELIGION. *Lent Lectures. By* HENRY PARRY LIDDON, D.D., D.C.L., *Canon of St. Paul's, and Ireland Professor of Exegesis in the University of Oxford.*

Crown 8vo. [*In the Press.*

AIDS TO PRAYER; OR, THOUGHTS ON THE PRACTICE OF DEVOTION. *With Forms of Prayer for Private Use. By* DANIEL MOORE, M.A., *Chaplain in Ordinary to the Queen, and Vicar of Holy Trinity, Paddington, Author of "Sermons on Special Occasions."*

Second Edition. Square 32mo. 2*s.* 6*d.*

www.ingramcontent.com/pod-product-compliance
Lightning Source LLC
LaVergne TN
LVHW010220110826
845151LV00004B/1158

* 9 7 8 1 4 2 5 5 2 6 3 6 8 *